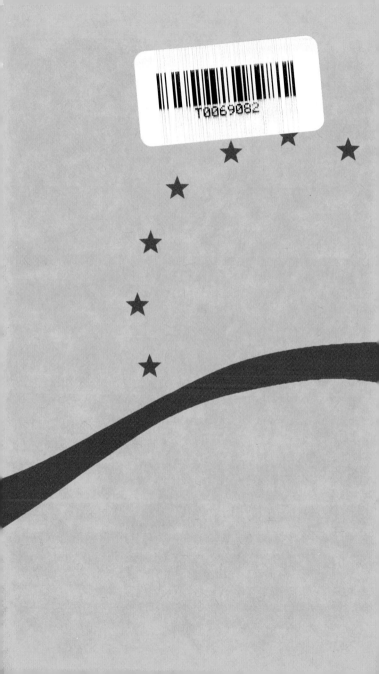

What Was Communism?

A SERIES EDITED BY TARIQ ALI

The theory of Communism as enunciated by Marx and Engels in *The Communist Manifesto* spoke the language of freedom, allied to reason. A freedom from exploitation in conditions that were being created by the dynamic expansion of capitalism so that 'all that is solid melts into air'. The system was creating its own grave-diggers. But capitalism survived. It was the regimes claiming loyalty to the teachings of Marx that collapsed and reinvented themselves. What went wrong?

This series of books explores the practice of twentieth-century Communism. Was the collapse inevitable? What actually happened in different parts of the world? And is there anything from that experience that can or should be rehabilitated? Why have so many heaven-stormers become submissive and gone over to the camp of reaction? With capitalism mired in a deep crisis, these questions become relevant once again. Marx's philosophy began to be regarded as a finely spun web of abstract and lofty arguments, but one that had failed the test of experience. Perhaps, some argued, it would have been better if his followers had remained idle dreamers and refrained from political activity. The Communist system lasted 70 years and failed only once. Capitalism has existed for over half a millennium and failed regularly. Why is one collapse considered the final and the other episodic? These are some of the questions explored in a variety of ways by writers from all over the globe, many living in countries that once considered themselves Communist states.

the idea of communism

TARIQ ALI

LONDON NEW YORK CALCUTTA

Seagull Books 2009

© Tariq Ali 2009

ISBN-13   978 1 9064 9 726 2

British Library Cataloguing-in-Publication Data
A catalogue record for this book is available
from the British Library

Jacket and book designed by Sunandini Banerjee, Seagull Books
Printed at Rockwel Offset, Calcutta

For

Aleem and Jordan Beaumont

who might read this one day

1

Humans often admire the spider's stratagem. There are more than a few tales of how the ancient heroes learnt perseverance by watching an individual spider at work. Where a lone spider can succeed, a lone human can follow. In more recent times, the comic-book Spiderman is denied the pleasures enjoyed by some of his rivals. Batman is secure with Robin; Superman's krypton-genes fail to immunize him against heterosexual lust for Lois Lane; even the Lone Ranger was provided with a tame Tonto to fall back on or 'get um up.' Spiderman is self-sufficient. He requires no support. Or so we are told.

I was reminded of the spider-myths while walking in the Margalla Hills in Islamabad last summer. Huge webs were in evidence that could not possibly have been constructed by a single spider. The helpful curator in the tiny office attached to the nature park has photographed and catalogued the creatures responsible for building these webs. She lists them as 'communal spiders', a sub-species that works in harmony in striking contrast to its individualist cousins. The use of the word 'communal' is not inaccurate, but slightly misguided given the geographical context—in South Asia, 'communalism' is used to describe acts of inter-religious violence, and a literalist might imagine that the Margalla spiders are somehow engaged in 'terrorist' acts. The word 'Communist' would perhaps have been closer to the mark, thought it might have cost the curator her job.

These Communist spiders are by no means confined to the hills of northern Pakistan. They flourish in the South American rainforests; in that continent, their large hammock-shaped webs are more accurately described as 'spider communes'.

For, these social spiders function as collectives, a free association of producers. They cooperate while hunting and constructing their communes; they share food; they have an effective system of crèches where they care for their own and each other's young. They have existed for at least half a million years and there has been no assaults on them by the more individual-oriented capitalist spiders. Could there be a lesson here for the human kingdom?

Capitalism appears more like a nervous disease these days than a triumphal, over-confident system generating unchallengeable ideologies to buttress and further its victories—democratism, free-marketism, human-rightsism—and to suggest to a passive world that the haves and have-mores have defeated the have-nots and the never-will-haves forever. There is no reason to despair, however, since the defeat of Communism has been beneficial for every individual regardless of his or her class location. Have-nots in the old sense, we have been told, no longer exist. In the new world order, the many benefit from their own exploitation by the few. All this has been accompanied by a stern health warning: no alternatives to the present are possible. The triumph of liberal capitalism marked the end of history, and all remnants, even of social capitalism, had to be wiped out. The hitherto strongly defended areas of social provision could no longer be regarded as sacred space: capitalism, backed by the state, would enter them at will and transform them for the better.

Utopia, together with all notions of collective activity and its misshapen Communist and socialist children, was buried safely in the family vault, together with the numerous volumes honouring the project that had been produced from the mid-nineteenth till the final decade of the twentieth century. Time, I think, to re-open the vault and critically examine its contents. The failure of official Communism in the twentieth century and the restoration of capitalism in Russia and China, with all that this has entailed, far from negating some of the premises that underlined the project in the first place, emphasizes their continuing importance.

In his most recent work, the Italian philosopher, Lucio Magri, stresses this aspect:

> At one of the crowded meetings held in 1991 to decide whether or not to change the name of the Italian Communist Party, a comrade posed this question to Pietro Ingrao: 'After everything that has happened and all that is now taking place, do you still believe the word "communist" can be used to describe the kind of large, democratic mass party that ours has been, and is, and which we want to renew so as to take it into government?' Ingrao, who had already laid out in full the reasons for his dissent and proposed that an alternative course be taken, replied—not altogether in jest—with Brecht's famous parable of the tailor of Ulm. This sixteenth-century German artisan had been obsessed by the idea of building a device that would allow men to fly. One day, convinced he had succeeded, he took his contraption to the Bishop and said: 'Look, I can fly.' Challenged to prove it, the tailor launched himself into the air from the top of the church roof,

and, naturally, ended up in smithe-reens on the
paving stones below. And yet, Brecht's poem
suggests: a few centuries later men did indeed
learn to fly.[1]

THE NOTION OF 'FREEDOM' emerged as a response
to slavery; the idea of 'Communism' grew out of a
need to challenge the wage-slavery of workers during the industrial capitalism of the nineteenth and
twentieth centuries. The processes were considered
analogous. Whereas a slave was regarded as private
property to be bought and sold in the marketplace,
the worker or wage-slave was property-less but en-
chained. The slave lived in shacks close to the fields
and plantations where he worked, dependent on his
or her owner for continued existence. The first
industrial workers lived in semi-slums close to the
factory or the mines where they were employed; in
many cases, these were owned by their employers
and tied to the job. Out of work, out of home. The
maltreatment of slaves led to frequent rebellions
from the time of Spartacus onwards, but the over-

whelming strength of slave states always determined the outcome. This remained the case for many centuries, until the first real victory won by slaves and former slaves—the triumph of the 'black Jacobins'— in Haiti, soon after 1793, when the French Revolution veered sharply to the left, an event that ignited hope among slaves as far apart as Brazil and the United States.[2]

The extreme working conditions of 'wage-slaves' further deteriorated as the Industrial Revolution of the nineteenth century spread and took root in western Europe and North America. Some of the finest descriptions of those early conditions, under which men, women and children laboured, are to be found in the novels of Charles Dickens, Emile Zola and Upton Sinclair. Workers responded to the oppression by attempts at self-organization and struggles for unity against the bosses. Even before the birth of Fordism, there had been virtual uprisings by weavers in Silesia and Lyon. (They were usually greeted by repression.) And there is a memorable account of a Lyon weaver walking to Paris with the aim of 'killing a bourgeois', one example among many of 'propaganda by the deed'. Simultaneous attempts to enlarge the suffrage produced embryonic trades unions in each craft and industry and, later, political parties created to represent the interest of the workers.

The first systematic attempts to codify the ideas that became known as Communism were born together with the modern proletariat during the early years of the Industrial Revolution—the technological leap that transformed the West (and Japan). Its results were what we can, in retrospect, describe as the first wave of globalization. From its continental launching pad, western Europe went in search of new markets and, in the process, unleashed a set of colonial wars and occupations and laid the foundations of new empires. The late eighteenth, nineteenth and early twentieth centuries witnessed important economic and political changes that were decisive in the formation of the modern world.

The seeds, of course, had been planted by an intellectual–political revolution: the Enlightenment and the French upheavals of 1789–1815. The tree of Communism was stunted by defeats, but gained height with every new upsurge. Aware of the spectre in question, the Congress of Victors that met in Vienna in 1815 mapped a Europe where dissent could be easily controlled. The Vienna Consensus would be policed by Prussia, Russia and Austria with the British Navy as a reliable last resort. On the intellectual front, Hegel, theorist of permanent mobility, strong proponent of the idea that everything moves, that history, itself the result of a clash of ideas, is never static (each idea producing its opposite) and that this dialectic, where past and present determine the future, is both inevitable, unpredictable and unstoppable, now accepted the end of history. The once dynamic 'world-spirit' had cast aside Napoleon's greatcoat and hat in favour of the steel helmets of the Prussian Junkers. A victorious Prussia had become the model state, the final resting place of the historical process. As we now know, this turned out not to be the case and many of Hegel's young followers, while using his method to investigate the real world, were finding his conclusions deficient. They began to challenge his basic premises and ended up turning the master's teaching on its head.

Ludwig Feurbach began this process: refuting the notion that ideas determined being, he insisted upon the opposite—that being determined consciousness. Another young Hegelian, Karl Marx, took the critique further by articulating the social and class differences within society as a whole. Might these have something to do with the difference in status between the King of Prussia, a Moselle peasant and a factory worker? They were all humans, they shared physiological and anatomical characteristics—but a social gulf divided them from each other, and those alive in the nineteenth century differed from those in the seventeenth, twelfth or earlier periods. Human beings were a product of Nature, but how did the differences emerge? It was not enough to say that humans were a product of their environment or that property was theft. What were the conditions that produced the ensemble of social relations that highlighted the difference between one class and another? Surely, Marx argued, it was this complex of contradictions that had to be analysed in order to understand the world. Marx and his co-thinkers were to spend their entire lives answering this question and, in the course of their researches, producing analyses of differing social formations since the beginning of written history. This history could only be understood as a clash between contending classes and their economic interests. Understanding history in this way was later categorized as historical materialism and, in some ways, remains the most important contribution of Marx, Friedrich Engels and the historians who followed in their tracks. It transformed the way history was studied, and Feminist and Black Studies owe a great deal to this tradition. And, because it is of lasting value, it will last as long as the planet.

WHAT OF THE *COMMUNIST MANIFESTO* (1848) that acquired the status of a sacred text even before the Russian Revolution? It was commissioned as the founding programme of the Communist League, a collection of mainly German exiles and a sprinkling of their Belgian and English supporters who met in London in the summer of 1847. The League's motto was 'Workers of all countries, unite' and the first paragraph of its constitution was self-explanatory: 'The aim of the League is the over-throw of the bourgeoisie, the rule of the proletariat, the abolition of the old bourgeois society based on class antagonisms, and the establishment of a new society without either classes or private property.'[3]

The Central Committee instructed Marx to produce a manifesto. A few months later, the docu-ment was still not forthcoming and a slightly tetchy triumvirate—consisting of Citizens Karl Schapper, Heinrich Bauer and Joseph Moll—despatched a warning note to the author on behalf of the Com-mittee:

> The Central Committee [in London] hereby di-rects the District Committee of Brussels to no-tify Citizen Marx that if the Manifesto of the Communist Party, which he consented, at the

last Congress, to draw up, does not reach London before Tuesday February 1 [1848], further measures will be taken against him. In case Citizen Marx does not write the Manifesto, the Central Committee requests the immediate return of the documents that were turned over to him by the Congress.[4]

The comrades were angry for good reason. Information was reaching them from several European countries of growing discontent among the people, especially workers against the 1815 Settlement. A democratic surge was expected any minute in Germany. Given all this, what on earth was Citizen Marx up to? To be fair, he was working on the document, but his perfectionism—he laboured long and hard when he knew a text was important—always led to delays. While he was busy, painstakingly refining each phrase and sentence, Marx and Engels had been engaged, for several months, in lectures and detailed discussions with exiled migrant German workers and intellectuals in London and Brussels, most of them members of the German

Workers' Educational Association. The original organizational model had been French revolutionary secret societies, but contacts with the English Chartists had revealed the advantages of open mass organization and public agitation.

Neither of the authors was involved in any frivolous pursuits, but the letter of warning (an equivalent of a modern publisher demanding that either the advance be returned or a finished manuscript) was sufficient to speed up the process. Marx completed the final text, with some help from Citizen Engels, in the first week of February 1848. It was published a few days before the eruption of the 1848 revolutions, first in France and then spreading to the rest of the continent. Though the *Manifesto* played no part in the preparation of, nor had any impact on, these events, its influence began to grow. By the time of the Paris Commune of 1871, the message outlined in its text was well established. The famous opening sentences became prophetic for the century that lay ahead, except that the spectre of Communism no longer haunted Europe alone but the world.

The *Manifesto* itself was the result of a synthesis: German philosophy, English economics and French politics framed the consciousness of its two authors.[5] A detailed commentary on the text is unnecessary— it deserves to be read on its own. (Eric Hobsbawm's introduction to a recent version is a tasty *hors d'ouevre* that serves to enhance appetite for the main course.[6])

In order to provide a thorough critique of bourgeois society as it existed at the time, Marx felt obliged to explain the evolutionary pattern of all human societies, the transition from one mode of production to another, since, in his view, the relations of production constituted 'the anatomical system' of every society and it was this that led him to undertake a detailed study of the workings of capitalism. Sociology and history had been mastered, but he needed the economics to lay the foundations of a revolutionary theory that would help defeat the bourgeoisie that had created the capitalist system via revolutions of which the English and French remained the exemplars. And as the bourgeoisie grew in the womb of medieval feudalism, so a new class

was developing in the womb of the bourgeoisie—
the industrial proletariat. Each system produced its
own gravediggers. The transition from feudalism to
capitalism had taken centuries. How long would it
take before socialism/Communism replaced capitalism? No time-scale was ever proposed by the
authors of the *Manifesto* but the inevitability of such
a process was stressed in such a way as to imply a
spontaneous explosion/transition, and mechanistic
interpretations became the vogue.

There is in the *Manifesto* lyrical praise of the
transforming capacities of capitalism—it 'has accomplished wonders far surpassing Egyptian pyra-
mids, Roman aqueducts and Gothic cathedrals'.[7]
The new wonders of the world were cited thus:

> The bourgeoisie, during its rule of scarce one
> hundred years, has created more massive and
> more colossal productive forces than have all
> preceding generations together. Subjection of
> Nature's forces to man, machinery, application
> of chemistry to industry and agriculture, steam-
> navigation, railways, electric telegraphs, clear-

ing of whole continents for cultivation, canali-
sation of rivers, whole populations conjured out
of the ground—what earlier century had even
a presentiment that such productive forces
slumbered in the lap of social labour?[8]

Underlying all this was a belief that, while the
bourgeoisie had carried through its revolutions in its
own interests, necessarily those of a minority, a triumphant proletarian revolution built on these foundations could go much further in transforming the
'realm of necessity' into the 'realm of freedom'. The
Manifesto was a broad-sweep document, and many
of its predictions were not borne out. For a start,
capitalism expanded mightily but without reducing
its heartlands—leave alone the colonized world—to
a simplified class structure of workers versus the cap-
italists. Britain came closest to that prediction, but, in
the rest of western Europe, the peasants and farm-
ers continued to exist as an important social layer.
And, as Marx recognized in his later work, even
those who sold their labour power were themselves
divided into better-paid workers, reserve armies of

the unemployed and nomad workers who moved from city to city. Add to that the difference of age, language, religion, gender and ethnic origin, and the notion that the proletariat was united for itself against its class enemy appears simplistic. Sociology was insufficient—politics was needed, and a party programme based on building alliances with the bourgeoisie against remnants of the feudal or pre-capitalist survivals and with the peasants and petty-bourgeoisie against the bourgeoisie. Unsurprisingly, all this led to debates as the Social Democratic movement began the arduous task of grappling with these and related issues.

It was repeatedly stressed by Communism's founding fathers that capitalism as a system could never be confined to a single state—that was not the nature of the beast. Marx provided a rich narrative of the birth of industrial capitalism. Seeded in the cities of mediaeval Italy, it grew in Flanders and Holland, spent its teens helping the Portuguese and Spanish empires and, aided by the English Revolution, came of age in England by the end of the seventeenth century. It was an interlinked narrative: without the needs of the Flemish artisans and traders in their urban enclaves, English farming could not have acquired a commercial importance. Had this not taken place, the Industrial Revolution would have been delayed. Once it happened, capitalism had no option but to become global and, since the system was based on profit, it could not exist without exploitation and its growth and spread could only create a set of contradictions that would help revolutionize the world. A strong idea, it became the basis for creating political parties capable of transforming the contradictions of the system into proletarian revolutions. The most extreme contradiction was, of course, war, and one of Marx's more gifted Russian followers would later describe the period that opened up after the First World War as 'an epoch of wars and revolutions'.[9]

Famously, Marx and Engels left no detailed blueprint of what a socialist or Communist society should look like, something that often led the more academically inclined among their supporters in the

West to stress that the real originality of Marx lay in the realm of philosophy and economics.[10] And not just them. Apart from Rosa Luxemburg, the young Leon Trotsky and Vladimir I. Lenin of the pre-1917 *State and Revolution*, few of those who came to power in Petrograd were inclined to elaborate on what Marx had intended when he spoke of the 'dictatorship of the proletariat'. The defeat of the 1848 revolution had led to reflections on the nature of the modern state. The Paris Commune offered a glimpse of what a socialist republic might look like in the upheavals of the future.

Marx's response to the defeat suffered by the Communards was *Civil War in France: The Paris Commune* (1871). Here, and for the first time, he sketched the contours of a proletarian state. A prerequisite, however, was the defeat and dismantling of the old one:

> The centralized State power, with its ubiquitous organs of standing army, police bureaucracy, clergy and judicature—organs wrought after the plan of a systematic and hierarchic division

of labour—originates from the days of absolute monarchy, serving nascent middle-class society as a mighty weapon in its struggles against feudalism. [. . .] At the same pace at which the progress of modern industry developed, widened, intensified the class antagonism between capital and labour, the State power assumed more and more the character of the national power of capital over labour, of a public force organized for social enslavement, of an engine of class despotism. After every revolution marking a progressive phase in the class struggle, the purely repressive character of the State power stands out in bolder and bolder relief.[11]

Marx considered the French Republic to be part of the problem. It had sought to buttress and utilize the repressive powers of the old state apparatus 'in order to convince the working class that the "social" republic meant the republic ensuring their social subjection'.[12] This apparatus was the spinal chord of the bourgeois state regardless of its form: parliamentary republic or imperial monarchy; it was what constituted the dictatorship of the bourgeoisie. The first priority of a genuine revolution must therefore be the dismantling of the old apparatus: 'The first decree of the Commune, therefore, was the suppression of the standing army, and the substitution for it of the armed people.'[13]

It is important to stress these texts by Marx. First, because they reflect his view of history as *longue durée*. The English and French revolutions had defeated the old regimes and created new model armies to serve the needs of the new states. How could a proletarian revolution do any less? Second, there has been a growing tendency in recent times to protect Marx from the disastrous aspects of the Russian and Chinese revolutions by presenting him as a kindly Victorian gent, interested above all in press freedom and literature and analysing the ebbs and flows of capital in the old reading room of the British Museum when not picnicking with his family and friends on Parliament Hill in North London. This is, of course, true, but should not be used as a mask to con-

ceal his revolutionary views without which he would
never have visualized a Communist future.

Marx regarded the embryonic political structures instituted by the Communards as a qualitative
leap forward and superior to even the most democratic bourgeois republic:

> The Commune was formed of the municipal
> councillors, chosen by universal suffrage in the
> various wards of the town, responsible and rev-
> ocable at short terms. The majority of its
> members were naturally working men, or
> acknowledged representatives of the working
> class. The Commune was to be a working, not
> a parliamentary, body, executive and legislative
> at the same time [. . .] From the members of
> the Commune downwards, the public service
> had to be done at *workmen's wages.*
>
> [. . .]
>
> While the merely repressive organs of the old
> governmental power were to be amputated, its
> legitimate functions were to be wrested from an
> authority usurping pre-eminence over society

itself, and restored to the responsible agents of society. Instead of deciding once in three or six years which member of the ruling class was to misrepresent the people in Parliament, universal suffrage was to serve the people, constituted in Communes, as individual suffrage serves every other employer in the search for the workmen and managers in his business.[14]

Nor could the Commune only serve the interests of workers; it had also to empower other subaltern layers in society:

The Commune was perfectly right in telling the peasants that 'its victory was their only hope.' [. . .] The Commune would have delivered the peasant of his blood-tax—would have given him a cheap government—transformed his present blood-suckers, the notary, advocate, executor, and other judicial vampires, into salaried communal agents, elected by, and responsible to, himself. It would have freed him of the tyranny of the *garde champêtre*, the gendarme and the prefect; would have put enlightenment by the schoolmaster in place of stultification by the priest.[15]

The Commune could also cancel peasant debts and offer genuine benefits to a peasantry confronted with 'the competition of capitalist farming'.[16]

The experience of 1871 had demonstrated how the middle strata could be won to the side of the workers: 'this was the first revolution in which the working class was openly acknowledged as the only class capable of social initiative, even by the great bulk of the Paris middle class.'[17]

The greatest achievement was that the Commune had come into existence, but there were other lessons as well:

> The whole of the educational institutions were opened to the people gratuitously, and at the same time cleared of all interference of Church and State. Thus, not only was education made accessible to all, but science itself freed from the fetters which class prejudice and governmental force had imposed on it.
>
> [. . .]
>
> But indeed the Commune did not pretend to infallibility, the invariable attribute of all

governments of the old stamp. It published its doings and sayings, it initiated the public into all its shortcomings.[18]

Never one to mince words, Marx was scathing about some of the leaders of the Commune, who included 'survivors of and devotees to past revolutions [. . .] They are an unavoidable evil: with time they are shaken off; but time was not allowed to the Commune.'[19] Nonetheless the experience was significant for the future:

> The multiplicity of interpretations to which the Commune has been subjected, and the multiplicity of interests which construed it in their favour, show that it was a thoroughly expansive political form, while all previous forms of government had been emphatically repressive. Its true secret was this. It was essentially a working-class government, the product of the struggle of the producing against the appropriating class, the political form at last discovered under which to work out the economical emancipation of labour.

Except on this last condition, the Communal
constitution would have been an impossibility
and a delusion. The political rule of the pro-
ducer cannot coexist with the perpetuation of
his social slavery.[20]

What may have appeared to be the case in 1871
was no longer so 50 years later. Frightened by the
success of the Russian Revolution, pro-capitalist
politicians in the West began to think seriously of
putting their own house in order. Social and political reforms were instituted, including the extension
of the franchise to women. Large sections of workers increasingly consented to this form of rule, one
of the reasons being the huge gap that existed between the vision of socialism adumbrated by Marx
and the social conditions that underlay the first revolution led by self-avowed Marxists: Russia in 1917
was an underdeveloped capitalist country where the
peasants constituted a huge majority. China in 1949
was even more dominated by the peasantry. Marx
had pictured socialism differently; for him, it had to
be based on economies of abundance. Russia and

China were both social formations marked by scarcities of every sort. The fact that the revolutions took place there and not in Germany, France and Britain created numerous problems on the levels of both theory and practice. The hopes of the founding fathers of the Communist idea were not justified. After 1848, Marx realized that the European bourgeoisie could not be relied upon in any way. No longer the leading class, as it had been in 1648 and 1789 in England and France, it was now little more than a 'social corpse'. So much for the bourgeoisie. What of the proletariat? Here too, the authors of the *Manifesto* seriously underestimated the difficulties of winning over the workers in the advanced capitalist countries to the revolutionary cause. The creation of Social Democratic parties had alerted both Marx and Engels to the problems that lay ahead, and, in their *Critique of the Gotha Programme* (1875) of the German Social Democracy, they expressed sharp divergences:

> And to what does the German Workers' Party reduce its internationalism? To the conscious-

ness that the result of its efforts will be 'the international brotherhood of peoples'—a phrase borrowed from the bourgeois League of Peace and Freedom, which is intended to pass as equivalent to the international brotherhood of working classes in the joint struggle against the ruling classes and their governments. Not a word, therefore, about the international functions of the German working class! [. . .]

In fact, the internationalism of the programme stands *even infinitely below* that of the Free Trade party. The latter also asserts that the result of its efforts will be 'the international brotherhood of peoples'. But it also does something to make trade international and by no means contents itself with the consciousness that all people are carrying on trade at home.[21]

There was an additional problem: the Soviet model as it developed was not universally attractive to the workers. Marx's strictures on the Prussian bourgeoisie after 1848 could be applied to the dominant factions in European social democracy after 1917. But, with social democracy's total capitulation to capital after 1991, it may sound anachronistic to modern ears:

> [. . .] without faith in itself, without faith in the people, grumbling against the upper class, trembling before the lower classes, selfish in its attitude towards both, and aware of its selfishness, revolutionary with respect to the conservatives [this was, of course, rarely the case after 1950—T. A.] and conservative with respect to revolutionists, distrustful of its own slogans, which were phrases rather than ideas, intimidated by the world storm, yet exploiting that very storm, devoid of energy in any direction, yet resorting to plagiarism in all directions, banal through lack of originality, but original in its sheer banality, entering into compromises with its own desires, without initiative, without faith in itself, without faith in the people, without a universal historical calling, a doomed senile creature [. . .][22]

2

THE AUTHORS OF THE *COMMUNIST MANIFESTO*, unlike many of their followers, did not think that their own work was immune to errors and misjudgements. Such a belief was alien to critical thought and they would have been horrified by the suggestion that their writings might one day be elevated to the status of a religion. In *The Eighteenth Brumaire of Louis Bonaparte* (1852), Marx made this unambiguously clear and what he wrote of revolutions applied equally to those who theorized them in the first instance:

> [. . .] proletarian revolutions [. . .] criticize themselves constantly, interrupt themselves continuously in their own course, come back to the apparently accomplished in order to begin it afresh, deride with unmerciful thoroughness the inadequacies, weaknesses and paltrinesses of their first attempts, seem to throw down their adversary only in order that he may draw new strength from the earth and rise again, more gigantic, before them [. . .][23]

What if they were incapable of self-analysis? Then they, too, would become 'doomed, senile creatures'—the fate of the party and state bureaucracy that ruled the Soviet Union after 1927. The collapse of the authoritarian state apparatuses—that denied civil liberties to their populations; expropriated all rights of association and organization; maintained a total monopoly over the means of communication; repressed ideas and resorted to crude displays of nationalism and xenophobia to maintain some legitimacy—was predicted by neither friend nor foe.

In his last published interview, written a decade before the collapse of the Soviet Union, the late E. H. Carr—doyen of non-Marxist historians of the Russian Revolution—expressed his fear that the re-emergence of cold-war ideology and politics would freeze all attempts to appraise the Revolution objectively:

> One need hardly dwell today on the negative consequences of the Revolution. For several years, and especially in the last few months, they have been an obsessive topic in published books, newspapers, radio and television. The danger is not that we shall draw a veil over the enormous blots on the record of the Revolution, over its cost in human suffering, over the crimes

committed in its name. The danger is that we
shall be tempted to forget it altogether, and to
pass over in silence, its immense achievements
[. . .] Of course, I know that anyone who speaks
of the achievements of the Revolution will at
once be branded a Stalinist. But I am not prepared to submit to this kind of moral black-
mail.[24]

Any attempt to explain or analyse Stalinism
and its heirs must perforce begin by outlining the
aims of the Revolution from whose bowels it sprang.
It may be difficult to imagine, but the hopes aroused
by the victory of the Russian Revolution in 1917
defy quantification. They crossed national frontiers
with ease and aroused the working class throughout
Europe. In Asia, the Russian events provided a
tremendous fillip for the burgeoning national movements against colonialism. In fact, without the victory in Petrograd, colonial independence might have
been delayed for another 50 years. The rise of neo-
colonialism after 1991—the break-up of Yugoslavia,
the occupation of Iraq and Afghanistan, the mas-

sive expansion of US military bases to over a hundred countries—was made easier by the disintegration of the Soviet Union.

The success of the Revolution had transformed the size of the audience for socialist ideas. Until then, these had largely been the preserve, with a few exceptions, of a minuscule stratum of intellectuals and workers in Europe. After 1917, socialism appeared as a practical possibility to millions of people across the globe. Empires felt threatened. Capital trembled. Social democracy split into pro- and anti-revolutionary factions. The fall of Petrograd was, in other words, a universal event. The spectre of which Marx and Engels had written in the *Communist Manifesto* had been brought to life. The rulers of Europe, who occupied large parts of three other continents, buried their complacency as their subjects became increasingly restive. Crowned heads had, of course, been toppled before, but those responsible for these acts had been the unwitting agents of a historical progression. Cromwell believed that he was guided by Providence, both when he was negotiating with

Charles I and after the stubborn and manipulative monarch had turned down all overtures and offers of compromise leaving only one solution open. Robespierre claimed to be acting in the name of abstract principle. Lenin was not merely the beneficiary of a different historical time, he was also the major leader of a political party that based itself on a new understanding of existing social forces. It was their materialist view of history that distinguished the Bolsheviks from all previous revolutionary organizations. They acted as the conscious agents of a rising social class and were determined (after considerable theoretical and political turmoil in the upper reaches of the party) to declare war on property and transform the entire social basis of the state.

When a short, bald man stood up in the Petrograd soviet after the February Revolution and, in reply to what was intended as a rhetorical question, stated quietly, without a trace of demagogy, that his party was prepared to exercise power, he was greeted by cries of disbelief and hoots of derisory laughter. When, a few months later, the Bolsheviks had won a majority in the key soviets of Petrograd and Moscow and launched a successful insurrection, his political rivals were incredulous. There was good reason for their amazement. Tsarist Russia had been culturally and economically underdeveloped. The multi-millioned peasantry dwarfed the tiny working class. Russia had 'fallen' because it had been the 'weakest link' in the chain of European imperialisms. The First World War had laid bare this vulnerability and the Bolsheviks had pressed home the advantage: Land, Bread and Peace were the three concrete aims of the Bolshevik Party that ultimately united a uniformed peasantry, reeling from defeats on the Eastern Front, with the urban proletariat.

Marx had insisted that a socialist society could only be based on an industrialized society that possessed the potential of being rapidly transformed into an economy of abundance. This would create the basis for a political order based on a radical popular sovereignty. Workers and others would have self-government in a meaningful sense for the first time, and this democracy would exist on every level of society: national assemblies, but also municipalities, factories and fields. Tsarist Russia was almost the polar opposite of such an economy. For this reason, not a single leader of a party that based itself on the teachings of Marx believed that it would be possible to construct 'socialism in one country'. Lenin was to stress this fact repeatedly after the triumph of the October Revolution:

> Both prior to October and during the Revolution, we always said that we regard ourselves and can only regard ourselves as one of the contingents of the international proletarian army, a contingent *which came* to the fore, not because of its level of development and preparedness, but because of Russia's exceptional conditions; we always said that the victory of the socialist revolution, therefore, can only be regarded as final when it becomes the victory of the proletariat in at least several advanced countries. It was in this respect that we experienced the greatest difficulties.

> Our banking on the world revolution, if you can call it that, has on the whole been fully

justified. But from the point of the speed of its development we have endured an exceptionally difficult period; we have seen for ourselves that the revolution's development in more advanced countries has proved to be considerably slower, considerably more difficult, considerably more complicated. [. . .] But [. . .] this slower [. . .] development of the socialist revolution in Western Europe has burdened us with incredible difficulties.[25]

The Civil War in Russia was won by the Bolsheviks, but at tremendous cost. The intervention of the Entente powers proved to be a failure, though it successfully bled the Revolution. Capital lost the Soviet Union, but it was able to limit the revolutionary wave. Bela Kun's short-lived Soviet Republic in Hungary, even if it had survived, could not have decisively strengthened the socio-economic base of the Soviet state. In the capitalist heartlands of the West, the ruling classes successfully deflected mass upsurges by granting important democratic reforms (universal suffrage) and loosening the straitjacket of factory discipline (an eight-hour working day). Where this was not sufficient, capital exacted a heavy revenge for Lenin's success in Petrograd. In Italy, three years after Lenin's remarks quoted above, the blackshirted brigades of Benito Mussolini set fire to working-class clubs and rapidly extinguished all civil liberties. Beneath the admiring gaze of Western politicians, including Winston Churchill, Mussolini established a ruthless capitalist dictatorship, providing Europe with its first experience of fascism.[26] Portugal, Germany and Spain were to follow suit and in that order. Fascism was the punishment which capital inflicted on the working class for toying with the idea of revolution. The net result of all these developments was the total isolation of revolutionary Russia. Had a German revolution preceded the Russian by a decade or more, might things have been different? It is an intriguing counter-factual.

Direct military intervention had failed to defeat the Red Army, but the Revolution itself was scarred by the experience: a debilitated economy, a war-weary population, the loss of a whole layer of the most politically conscious workers and mass famines were the inevitable outcome. The economic blockade imposed by capital succeeded in quarantining the Revolution. Stalinism was the outcome of these multifaceted processes. The preponderance of the peasantry; the weakness of the working class; the total lack of democratic traditions; the failure of the Revolution to spread to even one advanced country in the West; the deaths of Lenin and Sverdlov—all these factors grew inextricably linked. The result was a growing passivity and demoralization in the towns. The growing apparatuses of party and state absorbed many workers. In the conditions that existed at the time, this was an event of decisive importance: it led to a qualitative increase in the political and social weight of functionaries. The rapid growth of material privileges that this layer enjoyed relative to the average working-class family was bound to have an effect inside the party and state in conditions of scarcity. The growing disjuncture between theory and practice led to a debilitating process that came to an end in 1991. It is worth remembering that totalitarian capitalism that was embodied in fascism was defeated by a world war at the cost of over 50 million dead. The Soviet Union, with most of its leaders morally and politically exhausted, collapsed without any direct military pressure. The defeat in Afghanistan was costly, but not a determining factor in the disintegration. In China, the dismantling of the old system was more carefully organized with the reformist Communist leaders (who Mao Zedong had accurately described as 'capitalist-roaders') going down that same road but at their own pace and with the state firmly in control.

Lenin's last struggle, waged from his sick bed where he lay paralysed by a stroke and isolated from politics, was against this growing bureaucratization—he perceived it as a potential cancer that could prove to be extremely dangerous for a young, already deformed, workers' state.[27] This and the great Russian chauvinism against the Georgians became major preoccupations. He realized that changes were needed and, in his last political testament, demanded that Stalin be removed from his position as

General Secretary of the Party. It was a desperate attempt to reverse the course, but it came too late. Stalin represented the party bureaucracy and the real task was to reverse the institutional trends within party and state. In their different ways, both Karl Kautsky and Rosa Luxemburg, representing the centre and extreme left of German social democracy, had warned Lenin of the dangers involved in banning all opposition parties. It was a 'temporary measure' replied the Bolsheviks. And, as Slavoj Žižek has recently reminded us, according to one of Lenin's last texts published posthumously, Lenin appeares to have understood the scale of the problem confronting the Bolsheviks:

> Let us picture to ourselves a man ascending a very high, steep and hitherto unexplored mountain. Let us assume that he has overcome unprecedented difficulties and dangers and has succeeded in reaching a much higher point than any of his predecessors, but still has not reached the summit. He finds himself in a position where it is not only difficult and dangerous to proceed in the direction and along the path he

has chosen, but positively impossible [. . .] He is forced to turn back, descend, seek another path, longer, perhaps, but one that will enable him to reach the summit. The descent from the height that no one before him has reached proves, perhaps, to be more dangerous and difficult for our imaginary traveller than the ascent—it is easier to slip; it is not so easy to choose a foothold; there is not that exhilaration that one feels in going upwards, straight to the goal, etc. One has to tie a rope round oneself, spend hours with an alpenstock to cut footholds or a projection to which the rope could be tied firmly; one has to move at a snail's pace, and move downwards, descend, away from the goal; and one does not know where this extremely dangerous and painful descent will end, or whether there is a fairly safe detour by which one can ascend more boldly, more quickly and more directly to the summit.[28]

Lenin's death in 1924 made the 'temporary measure' a permanent feature of Soviet life, but only after an open struggle within the Party, the only remaining organism—the only legal party—in the country where political issues could still be debated on the leadership and occasionally at conferences.

How had it come to this?

Stalin had understood even during Lenin's lifetime that Trotsky would pose a threat to bureaucratic hegemony. His entire strategy from 1923 to 1930 was built around developing alliances that could isolate Trotsky and his supporters inside the party, army and youth organizations. Though the Left opposition waged a heroic struggle, its defeat was a result of an objective fact: the Russian working class was exhausted, and fresh replacements from the countryside had diluted the *élan* and consciousness of the proletariat. The party and state bureaucracy found in Stalin and his faction the ideal ally. A growing merger of party and state apparatuses would soon lead to the extermination of all the oppositionists. In retrospect, it is not difficult to see that the failure of Trotsky and Nikolai Bukharin to unite against the bureaucracy aided the process.

This coalescing of party and state bureaucracies was demonstrated at one of the last debates that Trotsky attended on the Central Committee of the Communist Party of the Soviet Union (CPSU):

> MOLOTOV: And the party, what do you make of the party?
>
> TROTSKY: The party, you have strangled it.
>
> STALIN: These cadres can only be removed through a civil war.[29]

The new 'civil war' was soon launched in earnest. All the mistakes that had led to the defeat of the Jacobins after 1793 were reduced by Lenin and his cohort to a single error: Robespierre and Saint-Just's inability to develop a political institution and maintain state power. During the first civil war, both Lenin and Trotsky were obsessed by not repeating the Jacobin approach and losing control of the state. Safeguarding the revolution was their principal priority, whatever the cost. And it was high. Suspension of civil liberties; summary executions; arrests without trial; and the banning of all other Soviet parties, the logic of which was to finally ban dissent inside their own ranks. A young, non-Bolshevik Trotsky had displayed some prescience when he wrote *Our Political Tasks* in 1904, and argued that substitutionism was fatal to the project of working-class self-emancipation: 'Lenin's methods lead to this: the party organisation at first substitutes itself for the party as a whole; then the Central Committee substitutes itself for the organisation; and finally a single "dictator" substitutes himself for the Central Committee.'[30] He later disowned the pamphlet but never completely. Acknowledging that party discipline was necessary, he also insisted that his remarks were accurate in defining the mentality of Bolshevik Committee-men of the period.

It is often forgotten in the West and in restorationist Russia that the first victims of Stalinism were Communist revolutionaries who protested against bureaucratic travesties of the revolutionary process. In order to stabilize his regime, Stalin was to kill more Communists and socialists than his absolutist predecessor, the Tsar. The question 'what is Stalinism?' was first asked in whispers by imprisoned veterans of the Revolution. The first political strike against Stalinism was undertaken by old Bolshevik prisoners in the Vorkuta prison camp, where the speech of Socrate Guevorkian exhibited an amazing combination of theoretical clarity and physical courage, two attributes that do not always go together.[31]

Stalinism consolidated its power during the late 1920s, 1930s and 1940s, but in changed social conditions. Politically, almost every non-Stalinist alternative had been physically eliminated and the Party itself had become an instrument of the bureaucracy. This had been made possible by flooding the Party with raw recruits fresh from the country. There were 430,000 Party members in 1920, but only 135,000 of these veterans in 1927 and even fewer 10 years later. Like their old Bolshevik leaders, they too had been consumed by the purges. Hélène Carrère D'Encausse has pointed out that:

> There were practically no Old Bolsheviks in 1929 and barely 130,000 members who had experienced in the Party the epic of the Civil War.

All the others had joined when debate in the Party had already been contained, when the spirit of discipline had already taken the place of the revolutionary initiative of the heroic years and of the criticism of the first years of the Leninist USSR. This, then, was a new Party, whose heroes, ideals and moral rules were no longer those of the Leninist Party. At the cultural level also, the transformation of the Party was very important; the newcomers were of a very low intellectual calibre and were completely lacking in political experience. The main criterion on which they had been recruited by the secretaries was that of their blind obedience to the Party's authority, which became the new conception of the *spirit of the Party* (*Partiinost*).[32]

On the eve of the Second World War, the majority of Lenin's Central Committee as well as the distinguished military leaders of the Red Army had been executed. A hired Stalinist assassin terminated Trotsky's life in his Mexican exile in 1940. The war years were to provide a critical test for the USSR as well as the bureaucracy. The industrialization of the

1930s had been a costly affair, but it had strengthened the economic base of the country. It had also resulted in an amazing degree of upward mobility for numerous workers and peasants. Many workers were absorbed into the state apparatus; many peasants obtained jobs in the towns. The mass purges had, not surprisingly, left behind a mass of vacancies. The bureaucracy thus imposed its will only partially through coercion. The secret police was a crucial pillar of bureaucratic rule, and its position of authority in the Gulag gave its bosses a new importance as well as a certain autonomy. Despite all this, the regime rested on a social base. The new Soviet working class undoubtedly felt that it had a stake in the preservation of this regime. The urban workers had by now become the dominant social stratum in Soviet society. Without their active support, the Soviet Union could not have survived the Second World War. The crude Slavic nationalism which Stalin deployed as the leitmotif to 'unite the nation' indicated the degeneration of the bureaucracy. It was not, however, an explanation for the incredible

resistance of the Soviet population. The Nazi occu-
piers did win some support in certain areas of the
USSR, but it could neither generalize nor build upon
this support. Nor was the regime overthrown by social
strata favouring a restoration of capitalism internally,
while continuing to fight the Nazi armies. All the
evidence suggests that the War was the single most
decisive test for the regime. It survived. The victories
of the Red Army at Kursk and Stalingrad were the
most decisive triumphs in modern history. 'The hopes
of civilization rest on the banners of the Red Army,'
proclaimed American General Douglas MacArthur
on 23 February 1943. There can be little doubt that
it was the Soviet resistance that prevented the whole
of Europe from collapsing before Nazism.

The negative features of the victory were ini-
tially felt inside the USSR. Stalinism was provided
with a legitimacy it had hitherto established over the
corpses of old Bolsheviks. In the post-War years, the
Stalinist seal was observed on every level: state, economy, culture, Army and Church. Unable because of
its peculiar position to develop its own ideology,

Stalinism transformed Marxist theory into a set of pragmatic rules. History was systematically falsified and rewritten; natural sciences were obstructed and research suppressed; women's rights were severely curtailed: divorce legislation was designed to encourage 'family life' and the right to abortion was halted; homosexuality was regarded as a perversion, although it was not made illegal. A thinly disguised moral code, reminiscent of Victorian England, was instigated at every level of culture and education, finding its most notorious reflection in Anton Semyonovich Makarenko's socialist realist trilogy *The Road to Life* (*An Epic of Education in Three Parts*).[33] (With a few changes, it could well serve as the Bible of the Boy Scouts and Girl Guides in contemporary Britain.) Stalinism became a synonym for a bureaucratic dictatorship, and its deadening impact gradually resulted in the establishment of an iron monopoly of information, politics, culture, theory, ideology, economics and science.

The Revolution had liberated virtually every oppressed and submerged layer within the old society. In the realms of art and architecture, drama and literature, agitprop and cinema, sex and morals, exciting and innovative impulses were experienced that had no equal before or since. Vladimir Mayakovsky and Vsevolod Meyerhold, Sergei Eisenstein and Vladimir Tatlin, Alexandra Kollontai and Anatoly Lunacharsky, all combined to impel the Revolution to reflect and articulate the enthusiasm of a liberated intelligentsia. One commentator, not known for his sympathy to the Revolution, has recently written: 'With the tolerant and sophisticated Anatole Lunacharsky in charge of cultural affairs and with a high proportion of Bolshevik leaders (Lenin, Trotsky and Bukharin) being intellectuals [. . .] it was taken for granted that the creative process was not amenable to crude administrative control.'[34] With the advent of Stalinism, everything changed. At the 1st Congress of Soviet Writers, Karl Radek, a former Oppositionist who had made his peace (so he thought) with the bureaucracy, proclaimed that: 'Joyce stands on the other side of the barricades [. . .] Our road lies not through Joyce, but

THE IDEA OF COMMUNISM ★

along the highway of socialist realism.'[35] Alas!
Radek's own highway was to terminate in a prison
camp where he died a miserable and unrecorded
death.

What was true in the realm of culture was mul-
tiplied a hundred times over in the political domain.
The victory of Stalinism marked a qualitative break
in the continuity of the revolutionary process. There
was, however, to be no regression to the free market—the breach was carried out essentially on the
level of the political superstructures of the state. The
economic and social conquests of the Revolution
were not simply preserved; they were, in reality,
strengthened. Thus, Stalinism could not and did not
develop an ideology specific to itself but, rather, paid
lip service to the writings of Marx, Engels and Lenin
while simultaneously ensuring their mummification.
Stalin's own writings were exclusively derivative in
character. A study of his texts in isolation from the
epidemic of terror that he unleashed is, accordingly,
a pointless exercise. A decisive hallmark of the Stalinist tradition has been that it is based on a lie. Thus

a study of the Soviet Constitution of 1936 (the so-called Stalin Constitution) reveals a document that, on paper, is ultra-democratic, but is never applied in practice. The same can be said of the character of many 'theoretical' texts that were produced during the Stalin epoch. The most bizarre demonstration of this can be observed in the names which some of the bureaucratic states adopted: the Democratic People's Republic of Korea and Democratic Kampuchea are the two most glaring anomalies!

It is now fashionable among historians hostile to all social revolutions (past, present and future) to deny that Stalinism represented anything more than the inevitable outcome of a socialist upheaval. It is almost as fashionable as it was in the 1930s for liberals and social democrats to avert their eyes from Stalin's crimes and denounce his opponents. Despite all this, it is necessary to emphasize that Stalinism was not preordained but the outcome of specific international and domestic conditions.

Ever since the Russian Revolution, there has been a vigorous debate on its outcome. After 1917, three theories developed which attempted to come to grips with the new problems that had been raised on a theoretical and strategic level. In fact, on no other question has theory and political strategy been so closely related as in analyses of the nature of the USSR. The oldest theory was proposed by the defeated Mensheviks, who regarded the seizure of power by Lenin and the Bolsheviks as an adventure. Russia was not sufficiently advanced to make a socialist revolution. The Mensheviks believed that only a bourgeois state was possible, given the low level of the productive forces, and only they could ensure that it would be a democratic bourgeois state. The Menshevik argument was developed in a more sophisticated style by the Austrian socialist Otto Bauer, who was in no doubt that the Bolsheviks were laying the basis for a state that would ultimately evolve towards a form of capitalist democracy. In a pamphlet entitled *Bolshevism or Social Democracy?* (1920), Bauer characterized Russia as a state evolving via an agrarian revolution to a bourgeois democracy. His advice to the Bolsheviks was to suppress the contradiction between the economic base (which he saw as capitalist) and the state structure and inaugurate a peaceful transition to a bourgeois republic. This view was based on an economic fatalism that gravely underestimated the autonomy of politics.

Amadeo Bordiga, the father of Italian Communism, developed a similar theory after his breach with Moscow in 1922: that the new state was an organ of emerging capitalism. He advanced some extremely valuable projections of what a socialist society and Communism should be, but, since the USSR was clearly not that, it therefore followed that it was not socialist. What Bordiga's syllogism obscured was the possibility that there could be a long period of transition from capitalism to socialism in those countries where the economic base was underdeveloped. Both Bordiga and Bauer did not attempt to classify the Soviet Union by inventing a new category; they merely tried to prove that it was a state on the road to capitalism. History has proved somewhat unkind to their theses.

Since the Second World War, new attempts at classification have been made. Of these, the most enduring has been the project of Tony Cliff and his followers, based essentially in Britain.[36] Cliff developed the view that the Soviet Union was a 'state-capitalist' society and that it represented the emergence of a new ruling class, qualitatively no different from the capitalist classes in the West. Cliff's arguments made it clear that the economic functioning of 'state-capitalism' was not exactly the same as capitalism. His position is therefore, in some respects, much closer to the theorists of a new mode of production than the Leninist definition of state-capitalism.[37]

The second group of theorists stated that Stalinist Russia represented a new form of oligarchy which was more regressive than capitalism. The best-known exponents of this view were James Burnham and Max Shachtman, one-time Trotskyist intellectuals in the United States. Burnham's *Managerial Revolution: What is Happening in the World* (1941)[38] became a cult volume during the first cold war (1948–68); the author was to end his days as a supporter of the extreme right-wing John Birch Society. Shachtman continued to argue that the USSR represented a totalitarian 'bureaucratic collectivism', but, unlike his former collaborator, did not move as far to the right. He defended Kennedy's ill-fated invasion of Cuba and was an early supporter of US intervention in Vietnam. Nor were these views inconsistent with his theoretical beliefs: if American democracy represented the most advanced political form on this planet, then there was nothing wrong or immoral in supporting its attempts to export this 'way of life'.

The third important theorist of this tradition was Milovan Djilas. A member of the Central Committee of the Yugoslav Communist Party and a partisan leader in the anti-fascist resistance, he developed his analysis of the USSR after the Tito–Stalin split and later expounded his views in *The New Class: An Analysis of the Communist System* (1957), another cold-war bestseller.[39] Djilas, however, refused to leave Yugoslavia despite spells in prison, nor did he recant his beliefs; till his death, he remained a partisan—albeit a critical one—of Western capitalism.

Thus, with exceptions, every theorist who sought to invent new modes of production and new laws of development to explain the complexities of Soviet society ultimately ended up as an apologist for capitalism. Many disciples of these theoreticians, we should stress, ultimately refused to follow their leaders—they remained anti-capitalist socialists, but the inconsistencies of their theoretical assumptions became apparent whenever they were confronted with a serious challenge in appraising world politics.

In striking contrast were the views advanced by the third and dominant theoretical school. Trotsky's study of the Soviet Union was started during his Turkish exile as he attempted to utilize the geographical and historical distance between him and the apparatus in Moscow in order to produce an explanation which remains peerless to this very day. Trotsky's theses are now dated in some respects, but his general approach represented a phenomenal advance for classical Marxism. It is not surprising that, of all his writings, it was *The Revolution Betrayed: What is the Soviet Union and Where is it Going?* (1937) that was to be challenged from all sides.[40]

Despite this, it became a reference point for all those who engaged in a serious study of post-revolutionary Russia. Trotsky defined Stalinist Russia as a society in transition with specific relations of production characterized by the permanent contradiction between the collective ownership of the means of production and bourgeois norms of distribution. (A view further developed by Ernest Mandel in a number of essays, polemical exchanges and books.)

The three features of Stalinism proper had grown out of the specific conditions that prevailed in the Soviet Union and Europe during the 1920s and 1930s. Stalinism was a product of the defeat and isolation of the world revolution, a development that it had partially aided by its ineptitude and narrow-mindedness. Accordingly, it came to be characterized by: (a) an iron monolithism on every level of the Party, the state and the international Communist movement; (b) 'socialism in one country'—a theoretical justification of autarchy which turned the writings of Marx and Lenin on their head with catastrophic consequences; and (c) the abandonment of internationalism and the global utilization of Communist parties as frontier guards of the 'socialist homeland' (the Soviet Union) rather than as vanguards of particular revolutions. This was formalized by the dissolution of the Communist International in 1943. A challenge on any of these three levels would weaken the foundations of classical Stalinism—a process that had begun even during the dictator's lifetime as a direct consequence of the choices opened up after the Second World War.

The triumphant march of the Red Army to Berlin was reminiscent of Napoleon's sweep across Europe. Whereas Bonaparte had authorized certain transformations, essentially on the level of the political and legal superstructures, he had not permanently altered the social and economic landscape of the conquered territories. What would Stalin do? The accords reached between the Soviet bureaucracy and the capitalist democracies at Teheran, Yalta and Potsdam are currently being re-analysed by Western ideologues as instances of craven capitulation on the part of the West. Such an approach is typically ahistorical, serving the needs of the new cold war, and it can be dismissed without too much difficulty.

The United States emerged as the strongest capitalist state as the war drew to a close, and it demonstrated its new power by firing a nuclear shot across Stalin's bows. The victims of this cynical display of realpolitik were the people who died or suffered at Hiroshima and Nagasaki. The atomic explosions established the new status of the United States, but they could not, on their own, solve the problems that confronted capitalism in Europe. It was not simply that the possessing classes had been (with the exception of Britain) gravely enfeebled, but that, in a number of Nazi-occupied countries, important sections of these classes had willingly collaborated with their German counterparts. Vichy France was the most notorious of this class-before-nation solidarity, but by no means the only one. In a number of Eastern European countries, the old ruling classes had either been weakened and damaged beyond repair (Hungary, Romania, Bulgaria) or virtually disappeared (Yugoslavia, Poland, Czechoslovakia) as a result of the collapse of their state apparatuses during the military defeats they had suffered in the course of the Nazi occupation and liberation struggles. In Greece and Italy, the Resistance had been dominated by the Communist parties and insurrectional upheavals were clearly on the agenda. The Western leaders were only too aware of these realities, and Yalta and Potsdam was the price they were prepared to pay for retaining capitalism in Italy, Greece and even France (where the situation was more complicated). Eastern Europe was accepted as the Russian 'sphere of influence'—a vague phrase which meant that Stalin would be within his rights to prevent the establishment of regimes that threatened the security of the Soviet Union. In this fashion, the West abandoned the old rulers in Eastern Europe to the military superiority of the Red

Army. The one country where 'influence' was intended to be shared on a '50:50' basis between the USSR and the West was Yugoslavia. Tito, however, had other ideas and his partisans were not prepared to make concessions to those who had been obstructing the anti-Nazi resistance. Stalin's attempts to persuade Tito to accept the restoration of a nominal monarchy ended in failure. Yugoslavia's revolution was indigenous, a fact of decisive importance in understanding the subsequent evolution of Yugoslav–Soviet relations.

The important question remained: how would the Soviet bureaucracy change the social and political structures of Eastern Europe? The indecision in Moscow can be seen if we divide Soviet policy towards Eastern Europe into two distinct stages. The first, a period of empirical solutions. The main accent of this phase, which lasted from 1945 to 1947, was on reparations and a pillaging of the economies of the Eastern European countries, while their respective bourgeoisies still held effective economic power. Capitalist production relations were utilized to rebuild the shattered Soviet economy. The second stage was marked by the Stalinist rejection of a US initiative. When the Americans hurled the Marshall Plan at a weakened and shattered Europe, the Soviet Union was faced with an unavoidable choice. The aim of the Marshall Plan was no less than the restoration, revival and reconstruction of a severely weakened capitalist economy. In order to push the Americans back into their own orbit, the USSR had to consolidate its long-term position in Eastern Europe. This could only be done by a decisive leap which qualitatively transformed the social and economic structure of the 'buffer states' and ended the process of milking their economies. The Marshall Plan revived capitalism in western Europe despite Washington's awareness of the potential dangers in this process. Rebuilding German capitalism meant reviving the old pre-War rivals of American capital. It was the existence of the USSR that propelled capital to act against its own competitive instincts. On the other side, too, the Stalinist bureaucracy was fully aware of what a transformed Eastern Europe could signify. For that reason, the social transformation of Eastern Europe (with the exception of Yugoslavia and Albania) was achieved not just at the expense of the old bourgeoisies, which was inevitable, but also by curtailing, limiting and even preventing any mass initiatives from below. Capitalism was destroyed overnight, but so was any hope of socialist democracy. The Stalinist model was imposed wholesale on Eastern Europe. While most of the countries in question were largely rural in character, one had a more developed economy than the USSR itself—Czechoslovakia. The imposition of primitive Stalinism upon an advanced working class led to disastrous consequences, highlighting the deep crisis in which Stalinism was soon to find itself. The Czech resistance had been widespread and popular; the Czech Communists were largely based on the strong traditions of the working class; the Czech people had welcomed the Red Army as liberators. They were not to escape the horse-medicine of the Soviet bureaucracy, a process movingly described many years later by French philosopher Jean-Paul Sartre:

Czechoslovakia could have been the first power to accomplish a successful transition from an advanced capitalist economy to a socialist economy, offering the proletariat of the West, if not a model, at least an embodiment of its own revolutionary future. It lacked nothing, neither the means nor the men; if genuine workers' control was possible anywhere, it was in Prague and Bratislava. To its misfortune, the manipulators in Moscow, manipulated by their own manipulations, could not even understand the idea of such a socialism. They imposed their *system* instead. This imported, disadapted model, with no real foundations in the country, was sustained from the outside by the solicitude of the 'elder brother'. It was installed as an idol— that is to say, a fixed set of unconditional demands, indisputable, undisputed, inexplicable, unexplained. [. . .]

Let there be no misunderstanding: the men of 1945 were convinced revolutionaries and most of them remained so, but the system forbade them the experience of building socialism

themselves. In order to change them, the experience would have had to take them as they
were; the system took them as they were not.
Instead of presenting itself as an open set of
problems calling for both a rational transformation of structures and a constant modifica-
tion of ideas (in other words, a reciprocal and
dialectical interaction of practice and theory),
it posed with incredible complacency as a gra-
cious gift of providence, a socialism without
tears—in other words, without revolution or
any contestation whatever. The tasks were already defined; it only remained to execute
them. All knowledge was already complete: it
only remained to memorize it.[41]

The decision to transform the social order was
a bureaucratic *fiat*, imposed from above. It did, however, provoke a certain degree of enthusiasm from
below, especially in the towns. Important layers of
the working class were prepared to give the new
regimes a breathing space in return for the important social rights that they were being given. Andrej
Wajda's sensitive and intelligent film *Man of Marble*

[*Czlowiek z marmuru*, 1977] is an accurate portrayal of the contradictory tensions that existed within the working class during the late 1940s and 1950s. The extension of post-capitalist states broke the post-1917 embargo on the Soviet Union. Simultaneously and contrary to appearances at the time, it also *weakened* the hegemony of Stalinism. 'Socialism in one country'—how was this possible any longer? Stalin perceived at an early stage that the success of the revolution in Yugoslavia and the assimilation process of Eastern Europe meant that there were new autonomous and semi-autonomous centres of power. The monopoly of the Soviet bureaucracy as the only basis of authority for the world Communist movement had been objectively broken. Tito's truculence and the final split between him and Stalin led to fears that Eastern Europe might follow suit. The purges and show trials of the 1930s were now repeated throughout Eastern Europe. The first anti-God was Trotsky. It was now Tito who was described as a 'Trotskyite counter-revolutionary', an 'agent of imperialism' and so on. The aim of the

new purges was to remove every potential alternative
to classical Stalinism inside the Communist parties.
The death of Stalin in 1953 halted the process, but
confirmed the dead autocrat's fears. The first outbreak of working-class opposition to bureaucratic
rule erupted in East Berlin, where striking workers
demanded basic democratic rights: freedom of
speech, press and organization. The revolt was
crushed by Soviet tanks. Meanwhile, inside the Soviet
Union, Stalin's successors were seeking to humanize
the system. Nikita Khrushchev's speech at the 20th
Party Congress (1976) was, despite its obvious flaws,
a devastating blow for Stalinism on a global scale.[42]
Within Eastern Europe, there ensued an uprising in
Hungary (again crushed by Russian tanks) and an
upsurge in Poland in 1956. The latter led to the first
major victory for a current that became known as
'reform Communism' and that brought Gomulka to
power. It was the triple failure of Polish 'reform
Communism' to deliver the political goods (1956,
1970, 1976) that led to the emergence of Solidarity
in 1980 and 1981, symbolizing the distance that the
workers had travelled since 1953.

The crisis of Stalinism was to receive a new and decisive blow in the Far East. The victory of the Chinese Communist Party in 1949 was the result of a protracted struggle against indigenous reaction and Japanese occupation, which had started in the 1920s. It could hardly be argued that Mao's partisans lacked mass support. In its own way, the Chinese Revolution was, in social terms, an almost direct reversal of the 1917 model. Mao's forces had mobilized the peasantry and come to power in 1949 on the basis of a gigantic peasants' upsurge. They had then liberated the cities, many of which had remained under Japanese or Kuomintang occupation for decades. While the peasants were fully mobilized, the urban proletariat was almost demobilized as a class until after the Revolution, which lent the Chinese revolutionary process certain specific features. What concerns us here, however, is the undeniable fact that Mao's forces made their own revolution in the face of Stalin's open scepticism and minuscule material aid from Moscow. It was only following the success of the Chinese Communist Party in 1949, and after several weeks of hard negotiations between

Mao and Stalin in Moscow, that Soviet economic aid was forthcoming—a crucial determinant in aiding the development of Chinese industry. When the Sino-Soviet ideological dispute erupted a decade and a half later, all Soviet aid and economic advisers were withdrawn at a stroke. The Chinese Revolution transformed the relationship of forces both on a world scale and within the non-capitalist bloc. China, the world's largest state, could not be treated as a Yugoslavia of the East. The phenomenal advances of the Eighth Route Army had, in practice, buried 'socialism in one country'. Moscow's hegemony remained unchallenged for many years, but subterranean tensions indicated that the multiplication of authoritative centres of power posed real problems for the heirs of Stalin from the very beginning.

The one organizational framework through which all ideological disputes could be peacefully settled no longer existed. The Comintern had been dissolved in 1943, prior to the success of the Yugoslav, Vietnamese and Chinese revolutions. The in-

ternational Communist movement had no centralized press in which all contentious issues could be
debated. This, too, was one of the legacies of Stalinism. Tito and Mao had broken in practice with
many aspects of classical Stalinism, but their ideological formation had been as members of the Stalinist family; they could never break totally with their
past. This meant that there was never any real
search for an alternative which might have provided
a totally different set of criteria for running the state.
Ironically enough, a Communist International was
needed far more at this stage of the world revolution than it had been in the 1920s, when not a single Communist Party was in a real position to
challenge Moscow's hegemony, with the result that
the Stalinization of the USSR was replicated with
ease inside the International and its constituent organizations. This dependence was symbolized in
1943 in the decision to disband, which was taken in
Moscow without even the gesture of convening a
World Congress. Such an action would have been
impossible if there had been even one other centre

of power. It would not have been possible for Tito and Mao to have been cast out of a Comintern without serious repercussions inside the movement as a whole. The fact that Mao never attempted to organize a new International revealed the extent of his dependence on a number of crucial ideological formulae of Stalinism. Both the Yugoslav and Chinese Communists had made their revolutions by breaking *in practice* with Moscow. The failure to break with Stalinism *in theory* was to create a tragic disjuncture in the revolution at the very moment of its success. The mode of organization, best expressed in the complete equation between the party and state, the monopoly of politics and information, that characterized Chinese society, was not dissimilar to the USSR in the late 1920s and early 1930s.

This raises a gamut of questions which have yet to be satisfactorily resolved. Is it the case that economic backwardness necessitates a Stalinist-type political structure? Is not a one-party state the inevitable outcome of a revolution in an underdeveloped country? Is it a pure accident that every single revolution has resulted in a monolithic state, with the very partial exception of Castro's Cuba? If we were to look solely at what exists today, then we would have no choice but to agree, however reluctantly, that the answer to all these questions must be a sad 'yes'. To do so, however, would be to accept an ultra-objectivist, one-sided view of historical development. This leads to a blind worshipping of accomplished facts and can be utilized to justify every disaster: Stalin; the purges; the so-called 'Great Proletarian Cultural Revolution'; the horrors of Pol Pot; the self-parodying Stalinism of Kim-il-Sung; the debacle in Afghanistan; and the saloon-bar quality of the shoot-outs in Tirana. To suggest that all these events were inevitable is to fall prey to a political myopia of the worst sort. In my opinion, all these horrendous occurrences could have been avoided— they were not essential to either making or preserving the gains of all these revolutions.

It has been argued that these processes were necessary in order to establish regimes that were intrinsically unpopular and could only survive by creating a dictatorship over the proletariat and poor peasants. This certainly applies to Stalin, who came to power on the basis of liquidating large number of cadres and members of the party that had made the Revolution. The cases of Ho Chi Minh, Mao Zedong, Josip Broz Tito and Fidel Castro are somewhat different. Could the Chinese Revolution have succeeded if the Chinese Communist Party had not commanded mass support? Why was it that the United States explicitly sabotaged elections in Vietnam in 1956 as agreed to by the Geneva Accords of 1954? Eisenhower gave an honest answer to this when he told a questioner that, if there were elections, 'Ho Chi Minh would win 80 per cent of the vote.' If Tito had organized a poll in Yugoslavia in 1948, whom would the people have voted for? The answer to this can be elicited from the fact that Tito armed his entire population in readiness for any attack from Stalin. Which US-sponsored dictator in the 'Third World' has ever done that? Why was Castro able to stay in power despite continuing attempts to overthrow him by the United States—economic blockades, military invasion, CIA attempts at his assassination and so on? The Chinese, Yugoslavian and Cuban regimes have survived over the years because of indigenous popular support, and not through the presence of a foreign army.

The weakness of post-revolutionary governments has lain in their complete failure to institutionalize mass participation and control in the political and economic life of the country. It is here that the distinctive ideological thrust of Stalinism has come into full play. Both Tito and Mao broke with the Soviet Union, but neither was capable of a real break on the question of implementing some form of socialist democracy. 'Self management' in the Yugoslav economy was not a fake, but could only have real meaning if there were self-management within the political sphere. Mao's demagogic appeals to the 'spirit of the Paris Commune' during the 'Cultural Revolution' did unleash mass mobilizations, but for the explicit purpose of resolving a factional struggle inside the Chinese Communist Party.[43] In either case, were the people given any real say in the reorganization of society? The 'model' used in virtually every case was based on a variant of Stalinist Russia. If that model had been a different one, there is very little doubt that the Third World revolutions would have benefited greatly.

To return to the Soviet Union. Even if we accept all the objectivist arguments for the unavoidable growth of bureaucratic power in that country, it is undeniable that the conditions which facilitated the rise of Stalinism have now disappeared. The USSR is neither isolated nor a backward social formation. The level of culture and the standard of living is higher than ever before. Every worker is guaranteed the right to work, and mass unemployment of the Western variety simply does not exist. The Gulag is a powerful but distant memory for the bulk of the population. Khrushchev and Leonid Brezhnev moved the USSR into a post-Stalin era since the death of the dictator 30 years ago. Despite the very real changes, Soviet society remains undemocratic, ruled by a bureaucratic elite which jealously safeguards its power and privileges. The USSR has not even returned to the stage which existed during Lenin's lifetime, especially in relation to intellectual and cultural freedoms.[44]

THE DEATH OF STALIN posed a fundamental problem for his successors. How should they rule this vast country and maintain discipline in Eastern Europe? In the eleventh century, the monk Nestor had bemoaned in the Russian *Primary Chronicle*: 'The land is large and rich, but there is no order.' Stalin's heirs set their minds towards establishing an order that would simultaneously dispense with primitive Stalinism, attempt to integrate all the crucial layers of Soviet society and preserve the monopoly of power which the bureaucracy enjoyed. It is in this context that Khrushchev's speech to the 20th Party Congress should be considered. Undoubtedly an audacious move, it scared the Party hierarchy which feared that it might lead to massive disturbances. Khrushchev went ahead despite the opposition of a majority of the Central Committee. The consequent breach inside Eastern Europe and the world Communist

movement marked the beginning of a profound crisis in Stalinism. Khrushchev had insisted that the
speech was vital to prevent an explosion from below
and offer some hope to the victims of Stalin. His primary concern was the Soviet Union. The 'thaw' was
accompanied by a determined attempt to weaken
social tensions by reducing differentials and improving the living standards of the majority of the population—a policy picturesquely described by the old
muzhik as 'goulash Communism'. This went hand-
in-glove with a systematic termination of the reign
of terror that had characterized classical Stalinism.
Political prisoners were released in droves and the
camps were disbanded. The security services were
slimmed down and deprived of the virtual autonomy they had enjoyed under Stalin. The arbitrari-
ness which had been a hallmark of the old system
was replaced by restoring the confidence of the de-
moralized and atomized cadres of the CPSU.
Instead of a terroristic monolithism, with every
move dependent on the whims of Stalin, a slow
move towards bureaucratic pluralism was under-

taken. Within the Party hierarchies at both state and provincial levels, discussion was encouraged once again and ideological absolutism discouraged—a new approach aptly summed up by Hungarian leader Janos Kadar's slogan 'Those who are not against us are with us.'

The bedrock of the post-Stalinist era was in the sphere of domestic policies. The political stability that characterized the USSR from 1956 to 1985 (compared to Eastern Europe and China) can only be understood by studying the steady rise in living standards. This point was made very firmly by a well-known Soviet dissident, Zhores Medvedev, who lives in London:

> The economic situation in the country remains below expectations, but is improving slowly all the time. There is no unemployment, but on the contrary a shortage of labour—which creates greater variety of job-choice for workers. The average working family can easily satisfy its immediate material needs: apartment, stable employment, education for children, health care

and so on. The prices of essential goods—bread, milk, meat, fish, rent—have not changed since 1964. The cost of television or radio sets and other durable items has actually been reduced (from unduly high previous levels). In fact, there is now an excess of cash in people's hands, and consumer demand for items which a few years ago were not deemed vital remains unsatisfied. So inflation does exist, but for inessentials. The result is that there are few real signs of economic discontent in the working class . . .[45]

This improvement in living conditions has not been confined to the dominant Russian nationality, but has extended to the population as a whole. The Brezhnev leadership was only too aware of the national dimension within the Soviet system. It is the Baltic Republics that have the highest living standards today—a Central Asian peasant is better off than a Russian collective farmer, and there is no qualitative difference between a provincial town in the Ukraine or in Russia.

However, only a crass economism could compel one to view the situation complacently. It is the existence of a bureaucracy and the *nomenklatura* structure of privileges that acts as a massive road-block on the path of any meaningful democratization. National tensions in the Caucasian Republics have not been lessened by the economic advantages they have enjoyed. In October 1980, there were massive demonstrations in Estonia. This coincided with a letter sent to Brezhnev by 365 Georgian intellectuals, including members of the Academy of Sciences, protesting against the 'russification drives' which 'lead to a gradual loss of the national rights of the Georgian people that were won in the struggle against Tsarism, contradict Leninist nationalities policy and constitute a violation of the constitutional status of the Georgian people'. These contradictions extend into the CPSU itself, where they fester, creating the basis for future explosion. How could it be otherwise when the Communist Party was written into the 1977 Brezhnev Constitution as 'the leading and directing force of Soviet society, the nucleus of its political system' (Chapter 1, Article 6)? Thus no serious discussion took place about reviving the long-extinct power of soviets, since that would have meant a formal structure of representation and periodic elections. This would have threatened the power of the bureaucracy by signalling the end of its political monopoly. The old Stalinist methods were humanized but not altered in any fundamental way.[46] By the time Brezhnev died, the post-Stalinist phase over which he had so diligently presided also came to an end. There were a number of major scandals involving corruption at a high level, and the low-productivity levels in the factories were beginning to produce new strains. Bureaucratic pluralism had given Party bureaucrats a security that they had not enjoyed under Stalin, but it had increased the gulf between the *nomenklatura* and the needs of ordinary citizens as well as enabling local chiefs to organize their own networks based on patronage.

More fundamentally, the Brezhnev era, with its relaxations on the cultural level and the considerable improvement in the conditions of life, has had an enormous effect on the post-War generations. Those born after 1950 have not experienced the traumas and fears of the Stalin period. This younger generation enjoys a self-confidence which is more reminiscent of their grandparents than of their parents, and it is bound to exert a new pressure (and on every level) for democratic freedoms and a loosening of the ideological monopoly of the bureaucracy as well as its capacity for social control. The very successes of Brezhnev have created the conditions for a new period of turbulence. The fact that the USSR is an advanced industrial society places its economic base in a situation of confrontation with an outmoded and primitive political structure. Even on the question of improving productivity in the factories, a number of liberal journals within the Soviet Union have hinted that some degree of workers' control will be necessary in place of the present system of 'one-man management'. An unusual poll of 900 factory workers throughout the USSR, carried out by the Komsomol in 1977, discovered that 'only isolated individuals opposed the idea of electing the factory executive' and 'some 76 per cent of those who favoured elections maintained that under such a system production would become more efficient, management would improve and become more re-sponsible for their jobs.'[47]

Yuri Andropov was elected General Secretary of the CPSU at a time when the worsening international situation coincided with the need for an audacious new offensive on the domestic front. His death at the beginning of 1984 delayed reforms temporarily as the gerontocracy re-established its grip, but a new General Secretary decided on *perestroika* from above. Visiting the Soviet Union in 1985–87 on several oc-casions, it was difficult not to be affected by the polit-ical and cultural debates that were taking place everywhere. I was convinced that the changes would lead to the transformation of the country from a so-cial dictatorship to a social democracy and, indeed, the model for many reformers was mid-century Scan-dinavia. I was completely wrong. Invisible social forces (invisible, at least, to me) were already in motion. A strong layer within the Soviet bureaucracy was hell-bent on a total restoration of capitalism. It wanted to make sure that it determined the composition of the new millionaires and so it happened. The old links between the most corrupt elements with the Soviet Union and organized crime were now to produce a new symbiosis of mafia-style capitalism. If this meant acquiescing to US demands and pressures regarding the break-up of the Union, it would and it did. Mikhail Gorbachev lacked the political strength or knowledge to understand that the United States was not a well-intentioned objective player in this game. Having recovered from the initial shock (which its ide-ologists and intelligence agencies—busy in stoking new cold-war fears and the threat posed by the 'evil empire'—failed to predict) as the Berlin Wall came down, it moved rapidly into action. While preserving its own cold-war structures, i.e. NATO, it accelerated the process of Soviet disintegration with the help of Boris Yeltsin and his gang. The results for the Russian people were disastrous as even a cursory glance at the statistics of social and economic decline reveal. The rise of Vladimir Putin as a new strongman was aided by the boom in primary commodities and permitted a degree of social expenditure that helped to restore some stability. (Is this the basis of Putin's popularity?)

Stalinism was presented by its apologists as 'socialism', the first stage on the long road to Communism. This theme was eagerly seized upon by the ruling classes in the West which sought to equate the socialist project with the crimes of Stalinism. This remains a central myth of capitalist ideologists to this very day. To state this fact is not to imply that it can be easily conjured away. The crimes have been too great, the confusion engendered has gone too deep, the resultant cynicism become too widespread in the European working class, to disappear at a stroke. No book, anthology, article or poem, speech or TV play can effectively challenge this equation of Stalinism (or its modified and muted successors) and socialism. Relief will only come with direct experience and knowledge that proves the opposite. The populations of both East and West will have to see with their own eyes a system that preaches and practises both socialism and democracy (political pluralism, freedom of speech, access to media, right to form a trade union, cultural liberty) before a massive shift in consciousness can take place. Such a society would not simply bury the horrors of Stalinism (and its Chinese cousins) forever but would also exorcize its ghosts that have haunted so many formerly colonized countries by providing a malignant political model: one party; a state that excersises its functions against its own population; a monopoly of information; imprisonment without trial, torture, etc. Ironically, the capitalist world today is beginning to find such a model attractive as well, but a centralized authoritarian organization of the productive processes, directed by groups independently of the will or the consent of the population, is not something that can last indefinitely.

A twenty-first-century socialism based on a socially just economic structure coupled with a radical political democracy would offer the most profound and meaningful challenge to the priorities of the capitalist order in the West, which triumphed largely because of the bureaucratic despotisms that led to the besmirching of socialism in the former Soviet Union. The price paid for the survival of capitalism has not been a small one: two World Wars; genocide against colonial peoples (of which the Belgian effort in the Congo during the early years of the twentieth century alone led to the massacres and deaths of over 8 and probably closer to 10 million Africans: no museums to commemorate these killings); the use of nuclear weapons against Japanese civilians (while protecting the Emperor who unleashed the war); the use of chemicals in Vietnam; institutionalized misery in the 'Third World'; and the threat of a nuclear conflagration that could obliterate all life on this planet.

Nor has the twenty-first century started well. The invasion and occupation of Iraq has, so far, led to a million-plus deaths, over 5 million refugees and the destruction of the country's social infrastructure. These deaths are, of course, noted by the citizens of North America and Europe, but do not impinge too much on their collective conscience. As I write, the United States is occupying Afghanistan with the aid of Britain and mercenary forces hired from private firms and privatized states.

In an essay written in *New Left Review* immediately after the fall of the Berlin Wall, the magazine's then Editor, Robin Blackburn, effectively summarized the scale of the defeat without seeing it as something permanent:

> The debacle of Stalinism has embraced reform-communism, and has brought no benefit to Trotskyism, or social democracy, or any socialist current. Mummies of Lenin and Mao are still displayed in mausoleums in Moscow and Beijing as emblems of an old order that awaits decent burial. However, today's moribund 'Great Power Communism' is not a spectre stalking the globe, but an unhappy spirit, begging to be laid to rest. Yet a socialism willing to confront history and to engage with the most penetrating critics of the socialist project could enable a new beginning to be made. Significant anti-capitalist movements still exist, some influenced by the Communist tradition, but they lack a programme that could take us beyond

capitalism. There are surviving regimes that call themselves Communist or Socialist, but whether or not they can point to real achievements (as can, say, Cuba in the fields of public health and education) there can be no doubt that they too require an even more thoroughgoing renewal and reorientation—one aimed not just at constructing a genuinely democratic culture and polity, but also at discovering a new and viable socialist model of economy.[48]

It was the real achievements of Cuba that helped the political changes that have been transforming South America since 1999: the Bolivarian leaders have come to power in Venezuela, Ecuador, Bolivia and Paraguay through electoral victories and not armed struggle. But these victories were the result of decades of social struggles led by social movements against the Washington Consensus. The political defeat of the old oligarchies in these countries has reawakened hope, at least, on that continent. The entire socialism of which Hugo Chavez speaks is a set of structural social reforms designed to improve the living conditions of the poor. It appears ultra-radical because the measures taken were forbidden by the Washington Consensus. In reality, the changes amount to a radical version of social-democracy, long forgotten in its homelands.

The restoration of capitalism in Russia and China, albeit in different forms, should inaugurate a lengthy debate on the transition from capitalism to socialism. After 1917, it was assumed that it would be a much shorter process than the shift from feudal and semi-feudal societies to capitalist modernity. History decided otherwise. The transition from feudalism to capitalism was a process that took nearly 400 years and accelerated sharply during the industrial revolutions in western Europe. Were the revolutions of 1917 and 1949 part of this same transition? Certainly without the leap forward in education and technology that came after 1949, Chinese capitalism would not find itself as strong as it is today, a veritable workshop of the world that has transformed the world market and is shifting the centre of gravity of capitalism Eastwards. Or are these changes in China a transition to a newer and higher form of socialism—a grander version of Lenin's New Economic Policy of 1922—as some apologists for the capitalist road argue on behalf of the Beijing regime?

What of the alternatives? With the post-1990 entry of capitalism into Russia, China, Vietnam, etc., politicians and global media networks crowed that the capitalist Cinderella had defeated the ugly sisters, Communism and socialism. The shift was experienced by a majority of the world's less-privileged citizens as a collapse of all anti-capitalist perspectives and led to despair as well as finding solace in religion and pornography though not always as a combination.

A new mood for change developed slowly: the Venezuelan Caracazo in 1989 was the first rebellion against the new order; Seattle came a decade later, followed by the birth of a World Social Forum to counter the ideology of Davos, followed by a set of mass social movements in South America. The dramatic collapse of the Argentinian economy led to workers' self-management experiments, factory occupations and district councils in Buenos Aires to discuss a different future. In Venezuela, Bolivia, Ecuador and Paraguay, the social movements challenging the neoliberal order produced governments that represented a new form of radical social democracy that seeks to combine state, socialized, cooperative, small-scale private and individual enterprises. These popularly elected governments broke the isolation of Cuba and obtained its help in constructing health and education infrastructures that benefit the majority. If Cuba, in turn, learned the importance of political pluralism from its new allies, the results would be beneficial.

What happens in Latin America is important for the United States. The backyard has moved indoors, and the large Hispanic population within US borders maintains links with its past. The effect has sometimes been negative, e.g., among Cubans in Florida, but there, too, the mood is changing. The social movements in South America challenged deregulation and privatization more effectively than organized labour has done in North America or western Europe. If adopted in the United States today, this model could combat an economy run by Goldman Sachs and build popular pressure for a nationalized health service, massive investment in education and reduced military spending, and against bailouts for the car industry and sinking airlines. Let them fall, so that a public transportation infrastructure can be built based on an ecologically sound and more efficient train service that serves the needs of all. Without action from below, there will be no change from above. That is one lesson that all sides have learnt.

There are others as well. The practitioners of Communism failed. The divorce of theory from practice had become a permanent fixture. With the collapse of the practice, the doctors of theory, too, became discredited. Since its birth, the Stalinist regime had been forging the hammers that would lead to its own liquidation. The process of de-Stalinization was not the result of pressures from below in the Soviet Union or China. It was led by men—Nikita Khruschev in Moscow and, decades later, Deng

Xiaoping in Beijing—nurtured within the system but who realized that the ideology of societies over which they presided had become a relic, totally at odds with the realities of 'actually existing socialism'. Feeling vulnerable and isolated from their own populations who they had oppressed for decades, they embarked on a reform programme that finally ended in the restoration of capitalism. There were no mass uprisings or even limited protests to defend what had existed. This fact spoke volumes.

And yet the older generations preserve some positive memories of the social dictatorships (including in what was once East Germany). They recall a state that was repressive, certainly, and perhaps even needed to be toppled, but they also recall a free education and health system, subsidized housing and electricity, limited but cheap food and the knowledge that their children would grow up in a protected world. The inability of capitalism to serve the needs of a majority was thrown into stark relief by the crisis of 2008. The beast can never get rid of its spots. For that reason, as long as capitalism exists the idea of Communism will never disappear. The German poet Hans Magnus Enzensberger once wrote a short poem titled 'Karl Heinrich Marx'. It remains apposite:

> *I see you betrayed*
> *by your disciples:*
> *only your enemies*
> *remained what they were.*[49]

3

SO MUCH FOR THE IDEA and the practice that derailed it so dramatically over two decades ago. But it still refuses to go away. I am in regular receipt of emails from postgraduate students working desperately hard for their Ph.D.s, and their questions invariably boil down to one: was the idea doomed from the very start and do I personally have any regrets for the time spent in the 1960s and 1970s of the last century promoting the revolutionary cause?

What I have recounted so far is hardly original. How could it be? Much of this was once well known, certainly within the labour movements. The last hundred years saw more books produced on the history of the rise and fall of Communism—and by both sides of the divide—than on any other subject. Recanters still carry on, trying to wash away any signs of the apologia they used to pen in younger days.

There is little that has remained uncovered. It is necessary to restate some of this history simply because it has been forgotten. History itself, as an academic discipline, has been under heavy fire for the last 30 years. Or, to be more precise, the grand narrative version of, and here too, as on the political front, large swathes of the global intelligentsia have led an undignified retreat. For many educated in the spirit of postmodernism, there is no such thing as a proper narrative—only fragments, all of which are of equal value. Surely this most recent phase of global capitalism, rampant and turbocharged, that has transformed politics, culture, sexuality and the economy, is a striking example of a strong narrative requiring a robust intellectual response—not wishful thinking illustrated by vignettes from various cultures.

Many Conservative historians disagree with this type of history, and correctly so. They are naturally triumphant since their side won, though the refuse of recent events—wars and economic crises—is clogging their trumpets. To their credit, they are still capable of producing a strong and engaging narrative. Niall Ferguson, Professor of International History, Harvard University, and staunch supporter of the Bush regime's push for world domination, provided a narrative of the 'success' story of the British Empire to use as a model. I made my disagreements very clear at a Macalester College Roundtable in Minnesota on the American Empire, when I debated him and his less gifted colleague, Michael Ledeen, who held the Freedom Chair at the American Enterprise Institute.[50] What of his opponents in the academy?

Alas, the dominant response to conservative historiography from within the academy has shown Centre-Left liberals at their weakest. Some have bought into civilizational theories, while others have sought to combat the Right by denying European primacy during the period of industrial capitalism and empires and, in the process, discarding a materialist analysis of world history. This is partially a consequence of defeat, but acting as cheerleaders to the non-European world by distorting history will not work in the long run—the scaffolding is far too flimsy. I understand why it might be tempting at a time when European culture is permeated with notions of 'defending our Christian heritage' that unite neo-fascists, conservatives and many liberals alike and throughout the European Union. But the creation of imaginary histories by ignoring the rise of social classes in the interests of official 'multiculturalism' will be seen for what it is: a conjuror's response to what is perceived as a deep disturbance in Western culture.

Take, for example, one of the more distinguished purveyors of this line of thought, Professor Sir Christopher A. Bayly of Cambridge University whose latest work (designed, partially at least, as a riposte to Eric Hobsbawm and other Marxist historians) is riddled with unsupportable claims that are defended by specious methods.[51] Clearly, if the Industrial Revolution barely happened, then the working class it produced must also be historically demoted—and it is. It was 'jostling for advancement' like every other class, and proletarian consciousness was 'a consequence of turmoil and revolution, rather than its cause'. And, naturally, those who overrated the workers were anti-monarchists. For Bayly, the monarchies were all doing well, and it was fluke rather than an underlying historical trend that led to their removal; European imperialism was not derived from economic needs but from nationalism. One presumes that the Dutch and British East India Companies that were the pioneers of their respective empires and who soon needed to raise troops to defend their gains were a figment of our imagination.

It is the emergence of agrarian and, later, industrial capitalism in Europe, and, with them, powerful states capable of building gigantic overseas empires and cultures capable of scientific and intellectual revolutions without comparison anywhere else in the world, which together gave the West a global ascendancy that has still not been bypassed. These are historical realities that give no moral advantage to the region that once displayed them. To respond to all this with what is essentially a defence of relativism is pathetic. Bayly's account is little more than the needs of his own epoch reproduced in history

The merging of Centre-Left and Centre-Right ideologies in the academy reflects the current needs of the political realm in the West. The growing tendency here is toward politico-economic uniformity and intellectual conformism. Britain is a glaring example, but not the only one. Tony Blair and Gordon Brown mimicked Margaret Thatcher, but boasted of doing better than her when it came to serving the interests of the rich—and they did. Income disparities are higher now than under the Conservatives. It appears that all that the Conservative leaders can do is mimic New Labour and promise they will be less corrupt and safeguard civil liberties more forcefully.

In France, the right-wing President Nicolas Sarkozy proclaimed a similar unity of thought with his defeated rivals and invited former Centre-Left ministers into his government, making Bernard Kouchner his Foreign Minister in an attempt to stress the *nouvelle politique san frontiers*. Germany is ruled by a coalition of Christian and Social Democrats. Italy first witnessed the transformation of Europe's largest Communist Party into a Democratic Party. (The name is not accidental, and 'change we can believe in' was its motto in the last general elections as well, when we witnessed the self-destruction of the Centre and the far Left that had served in a coalition. They were outmanoeuvred and outsmarted by an entertaining, incredibly rich businessman, a former crooner, Silvio Berlusconi, who owns a bulk of the private media and who built himself a political movement with the backing of Northern Italian chauvinists and a direct political heir of Mussolini.) In the United States, too, the Obama administration preserves strong elements of continuity with its predecessor, especially in crucially important fields of the economy and the empire. The cultural shift is to be welcomed, but how deep its impact will be remains to be seen. Comparisons with the New Deal administration are far-fetched.

Capitalism remains an economic model that, whatever form it takes, produces misery and despair unless it feels permanently threatened from below or by obviously superior alternatives, which is certainly not the case at the moment.

In *Planet of Slums: Urban Involution and the Informal Working Class* (2004), Mike Davis, has underlined the trends in contemporary capitalism that have led via the deregulation of agriculture to an urbanism de-linked from industrialization:

> From Karl Marx to Max Weber, classical the-ory believed that the great cities of the future would follow in the industrializing footsteps of Manchester, Berlin and Chicago—and indeed Los Angeles, São Paulo, Pusan and, today, Ciu-dad Juárez, Bangalore and Guangzhou, have roughly approximated this canonical trajectory. Most cities of the South, however, more closely resemble Victorian Dublin, which, as Emmet Larkin has stressed, was unique amongst 'all the

slumdoms produced in the western world in the nineteenth century . . . [because] its slums were not a product of the industrial revolution. Dublin, in fact, suffered more from the problems of de-industrialization than industrialization between 1800 and 1850.'[52]

Likewise Kinshasa, Khartoum, Dar es Salaam, Guayaquil, and Lima continue to grow prodigiously despite ruined import-substitution industries, shrunken public sectors and downwardly mobile middle classes. The global forces 'pushing' people from the countryside—mechanization in Java and India, food imports in Mexico, Haiti, and Kenya, civil war and drought throughout Africa, and everywhere the consolidation of small holdings into large ones and the competition of industrial-scale agribusiness—seem to sustain urbanization even when the 'pull' of the city is drastically weakened by debt and depression. As a result, rapid urban growth in the context of structural adjustment, currency devaluation and state retrenchment has been an inevitable recipe for the mass production of slums. Much of the urban world, as a result, is rushing backwards to the age of Dickens.[53]

The new slums, contrary to the apologists of the system, are not the result of 'bad governance' or 'failed states' but the outcome of 'the brutal tectonics' of neoliberal capitalism and its priorities. And nor, incidentally, should they be regarded as reflecting the growth of 'international civil society'. Two-fifths of the workers in the developing world are low paid, without recourse to law or trades unions and engaged in 'informal work' that is by its very nature irregular and dependent on the reserve army of the unemployed. Even a cursory visit to the slumlands of Mumbai and Karachi is to return to the worlds so vividly described by Charles Dickens, Émile Zola and Maxim Gorky.

Giovanni Arrighi, who died in 2009, described in stinging detail the conditions that prevail in Africa and their cause. Like Davis, he laid the responsibility largely on the shoulders of the financial institutions in charge of implementing the Washington Consensus:

In 1975, the regional GNP per capita of Sub-Saharan Africa stood at 17.6 per cent of 'world' per capita GNP; by 1999, it had dropped to 10.5 per cent. Relative to overall Third World trends, Sub-Saharan health, mortality and adult-literacy levels have deteriorated at comparable rates. Life expectancy at birth now stands at 49 years, and 34 per cent of the region's population are classified as undernourished. African infant-mortality rates were 107 per 1,000 live births in 1999, compared to 69 for South Asia and 32 for Latin America. Nearly 9 per cent of Sub-Saharan 15 to 49-year-olds are living with HIV/AIDS—a figure that soars above those of other regions. Tuberculosis cases stand at 121 per 100,000 people; respective figures for South Asia and Latin America are 98 and 45.[54]

In *The Shock Doctrine: The Rise of Disaster Capitalism* (2007), Naomi Klein has demonstrated with facts and figures how what she refers to as 'disaster capitalism' has gained from natural and man-made disasters, highlighting New Orleans and Iraq and how both were used for the benefit of the market rather than of the ordinary people.[55] The result is unsurprising. She anticipated the obloquy and denigration this book would encounter from the dominant culture and she was right. She fought back, refusing to yield the argument to the apologists and defenders of the system.

There is an increasing inequality of global income-distribution. This is nothing new, but, until the Wall Street collapse of 2008, any strong critique of globalization was usually ignored and such writers traduced in the mainstream media. During the first half of the last century, for example, 'development' per se was said to be the way forward regardless of all else, a view criticized by R. H. Tawney, a British Labour Party intellectual, as nothing more than 'tadpole philosophy':

> It is possible that intelligent tadpoles reconcile themselves to the inconveniences of their position, by reflecting that, though most of them will live and die as tadpoles and nothing more, the more fortunate of the species will one day

shed their tails, distend their mouths and stomachs, hop nimbly on to dry land, and croak addresses to their former friends on the virtues by means of which tadpoles of character and capacity can rise to be frogs. This conception of society may be described, perhaps, as the Tadpole Philosophy, since the consolation which it offers for social evils consists in the statement that exceptional individuals can succeed in evading them . . . And what a view of human life such an attitude implies! As though opportunities for talents to rise could be equalized in a society where circumstances surrounding it from birth are themselves unequal! As though, if they could, it were natural and proper that the position of the mass of mankind should permanently be such that they can attain civilization only by escaping from it! As though the noblest use of exceptional powers were to scramble to shore, undeterred by the thought of drowning companions![56]

How can anyone regret the struggle for socialism that was waged in the last century, despite its outcome? The aim was to shatter the fortresses of stupidity, tyranny and oppression. On a personal level, I remain proud of what we argued for and against. It was not just people on the Left who put *Das Kapital* on the bestseller list in Germany after the collapse of the Wall-Street hegemony in 2008. Everyone wanted to understand the inner working of capitalism.

I rarely related to Marxism as a secular religion, but, rather, as a body of ideas designed to understand and transform the world. The very thought of a 'secular faith' would have been regarded with distaste and contempt by Marx and his comrades. It was ridiculous to imagine, and this was a common weakness in the decades that followed the Russian Revolution, that a debate could be resolved with a quotation from Marx or Lenin or Mao or anyone else. That was reducing a way of looking at the world to 'primitive magic' and to creating totems and taboos that became the hallmark of Stalinism. It also affected some of its more radical opponents who had different totems and taboos.

We have to take a long view of the historical process. The transition from feudalism to capitalism took centuries. Why did we imagine that the transition to socialism, that required a far more radical transformation since the threat to bourgeois society from socialism is far greater than that ever posed by capital to the landed aristocracy, would be swifter? The earlier transition was also the result of violent clashes: the Dutch Revolts of the sixteenth century that came to fruition after over half a century of violent struggle; followed by the English Revolution of the seventeenth century; the US War of Independence and the French Revolution in the eighteenth; the movements for German and Italian unification and the defeat of the Shogunate in Japan in the nineteenth. All these produced periods of dictatorships: Cromwell, Robespierre and Napoleon. Democracy, in any meaningful sense, came much later, 500 years later, when women were granted the vote after the First World War and the children and grandchildren of slaves in the United States were still fighting for the right to be registered in order to vote in the 1960s.

The second transition, too, produced a period of dictatorship: Lenin, Stalin and Mao. Why should the collapse of the old social dictatorships in Russia and China, and their replacement by capitalism, not be seen as part of a long transition whose ultimate destination is presently invisible?

The light is dim, but it hasn't been completely extinguished by the storms of recent decades. It might well burn bright again, sooner than imagined. For, as long as contemporary capitalism, a system based on exploitation and inequality and recurring crises, not to mention its impact on the fragile ecology of the planet, continues to exist, the possibility of anti-capitalist movements taking power cannot be ruled out. Viewed in this perspective, I remain an intransigent socialist and my ideas owe a great deal to the early founders of the socialist and Communist movements. Marx's thought was not an evil spirit that created a materialist hell and perished—it is a philosophy that seeks to explain the contradictions that exist in our world, something that religions can never do. That is why it can never be consigned to oblivion. For, the great task remains. A moneyed aristocracy rules large parts of the world via tame politicians of every hue. The duels between the possessors and the disposssesed continue, taking new forms. The mistakes of the twentieth century have to be learnt and transcended. Capitalism has failed to do so. Socialists must.

August 2009

And how shall it be then when these are gone?
    What else shall ye lack
when ye lack masters? Ye shall not lack for the
    fields ye have tilled,
nor the houses ye have built, nor the cloth ye have
    woven; all these
shall be yours, and whatso ye will of all that the
    earth beareth; then
shall no man mow the deep grass for another,
    while his own kine lack
cow-meat; and he that soweth shall reap, and the
    reaper shall eat in
fellowship the harvest that in fellowship he hath
    won; and he that
buildeth a house shall dwell in it with those that he
    biddeth of his
free will; and the tithe barn shall garner the wheat
    for all men to eat

of when the seasons are untoward, and the rain-
    drift hideth the sheaves
in August; and all shall be without money and
    without price.
Faithfully and merrily then shall all men keep the
    holidays of the
Church in peace of body and joy of heart. And
    man shall help man, and
the saints in heaven shall be glad, because men no
    more fear each
other; and the churl shall be ashamed, and shall
    hide his churlishness
till it be gone, and he be no more a churl; and
    fellowship shall be
established in heaven and on the earth.

A Dream of John Ball (1888)
William Morris

Notes

1 Lucio Magri, 'The Tailor of Ulm', *New Left Review*, 51 (May–June 2008): 47–62.

2 *The Black Jacobins* by C. L. R. James (London: Secker and Warburg, 1938) provides a historical account that has yet to be bettered.

3 See David Riazanov, *Karl Marx and Fredrich Engels: An Introduction to their Lives and Work* (Joshua Kunitz trans.) (New York: Monthly Review Press, 1973 [1927; first published 1937]), p. 74. Also available at: www.marxists.org/archive/riazanov/works/1927-ma/ch04.htm

4 Ibid., p 78.

5 Somewhat different from the PPE—Politics, Philosophy and Economics—combo offered by Oxford University during my stay.

6 Karl Marx and Friedrich Engels, *The Communist Manifesto* (with an introduction by Eric Hobsbawm) (London: Verso, 1998).

7 Karl Marx and Friedrich Engels, 'Bourgeois and Proletarians', in *The Communist Manifesto* (Samuel Moore trans.) (London: Penguin, 1967), pp. 80–6.

8 Ibid.

9   The first Russian translation of the *Manifesto* was by Mikhail Bakunin, who later became a founding father of Anarchism.

10 Were this the case, then the *Manifesto* and numerous other essays and pamphlets containing political texts and some prescriptions become historical curiosities.

11 Karl Marx and Vladimir I. Lenin, *Civil War in France: The Paris Commune* (2nd revised edition; New York: International Publishers Co., 1988 [1871]), pp. 54–5. Also available at: marxists.org/archive/marx/works/1871/civil-war-france/index.htm

12 Ibid.

13 Ibid., p. 57.

14 Ibid., pp. 57–8, emphasis in original.

15 Ibid., pp. 63–4.

16 Ibid., p. 64.

17 Ibid., p. 62.

18 Ibid., pp. 58, 67.

19 Ibid., p. 67.

20 Ibid., p. 60.

21 Karl Marx and Friedrich Engels, *Critique of the Gotha Programme*, in *Selected Works* (Moscow: Progress

Publishers, 1970), VOL. 3, pp. 13–30, emphasis in original. Also available at: www.marxists.org/archive/marx/works/1875/gotha/index.htm

22 Riazanov, *Karl Marx and Fredrich Engels*, p. 96. Also available at: www.workers.org/cm/ch05.html

23 Karl Marx, *The Eighteenth Brumaire of Louis Bonaparte* (New York: International Publishers, 1963 [1852]), p. 19.

24 E. H. Carr, 'The USSR and the West', *New Left Review*, 1(111) (September 1978): 25–36 .

25 Vladimir I. Lenin, 'Seventh All-Russia Congress of Soviets (December 5–9 1919)', in *Collected Works*, VOL. 30 (Moscow: Progress Publishers, 1965), pp. 205–52; see p. 207. Also available at: www.marxists. org/archive/lenin/works/1919/dec/05.htm

26 Winston Churchill told Italian journalists in Rome in 1927 that, 'if I had been an Italian, I am sure I would have been wholeheartedly with you from start to finish in your triumphant struggle against the bestial appetites and passions of Leninism.' Quoted in Ralph Miliband, *Capitalist Democracy in Britain* (Oxford: Oxford University Press, 1983), p. 47. Lord Reith, the hallowed father-figure of the BBC, was another admirer of Mussolini and Hitler!

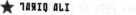
27 The most precise account of this last critical phase of Lenin's life is contained in Moshe Lewin, *Lenin's Last Struggle* (London: Faber and Faber, 1968).

28 Vladimir I. Lenin, 'Notes of a Publicist', in *Collected Works*, VOL. 33 (Moscow: Progress Publishers, 1966), pp. 204–07. Quoted in Slavoj Žižek, 'How to Begin from the Beginning', *New Left Review*, 57 (May–June 2009): 43–55 .

29 This exchange took place on 1 August 1927 and is quoted in Ernest Mandel, *Trotsky: A Study in the Dynamic of His Thought* (London: New Left Books, 1979), p. 81.

30 Leon Trotsky, *Our Political Tasks* (London: New Park Publications, 1979 [1904]).

31 See 'M.B.', 'Trotskyists at Vorkuta: An Eyewitness Report', *International Socialist Review* (Summer 1963): 206–16.

32 Hélène Carrère D'Encausse, *Stalin: Order Through Terror* (London: Longman, 1981). Quoted in Tariq Ali (ed.), *The Impact of the Stalinist Legacy: Its Impact on Twentieth-century World Politics* (London: Penguin, 1984), p. 12.

33 Anton Semyonovich Makarenko, *The Road to Life* (*An*

Epic of Education in Three Parts) (Moscow: Foreign Languages Publishing House, 1951).

34 Max Hayward, 'Literature in the Soviet Period (1917–1975)', in Robert Auty and Dimitri Obolensky (eds), *Companion to Russian Studies, Volume 2: An Introduction to Russian Language and Literature* (Cambridge: Cambridge University Press, 1976). Quoted in Ali (ed.), *The Impact of the Stalinist Legacy*, p. 14.

35 Quoted in Ali (ed.), *The Impact of the Stalinist Legacy*, p. 14. Radek's servility may well have been tongue-in-cheek, though the cultured old Bolshevik had become a time-server. The most notorious thought-policeman was Andrei Zhdanov, Stalin's Culture Minister, who, in the Charter of the Union of Soviet Writers (1934), was to describe his literary theories thus:

> Comrade Stalin described our writers as 'engineers of human minds'. What does it mean? What duties does this title impose on you? It means that truthfulness and historical concreteness of artistic depiction must be combined with the task of ideological remoulding and re-education of the toiling people in the spirit of

socialism. This method in fiction and in literary criticism is what we call Socialist Realism. (Quoted in Ali, ed., *The Impact of the Stalinist Legacy*, p. 28.)

36 Tony Cliff was the pen name of Ygael Gluckstein, a Palestinian Marxist, who settled in Britain after the Second World War. Cliff was to break with Trotskyist orthodoxy in the early 1950s and found the International Socialists, the forerunners of the British Socialist Workers' Party. His best-known work, *Russia: A Marxist Analysis* (London: Michael Kidron, 1955), has gone through several editions. In sharp contrast to James Burnham, Max Shachtman and Milovan Djilas, Cliff remained an intransigent revolutionary committed to the victory of socialism.

37 For Lenin, state-capitalism did not refer to a new socio-economic formation but to a mode of functioning of capitalism under the control of a workers' state.

38 James Burnham, *The Managerial Revolution: What is Happening in the World* (New York: John Day Co., 1941).

39 Milovan Djilas, *The New Class: An Analysis of the Communist System* (New York: Fredctick A Praeger, Inc., 1957).

40 Leon Trotsky, *The Revolution Betrayed: What is the Soviet Union and Where is it Going?* (New York: Pathfinder, 1972 [1937]).

41 Jean-Paul Sartre, 'Czechoslovakia: The Socialism That Came In from The Cold', in *Between Existentialism and Marxism* (London: New Left Books, 1974), pp. 89–90.

42 Nikita Khrushchev, *Secret Speech: Delivered to the Closed Session of the Twentieth Congress of the Communist Party of the Soviet Union* (Nottingham: Spokesman Books, for the Bertrand Russell Peace Foundation, 1976).

43 See Livio Maitan, *Party, Army and Masses in China: A Marxist Interpretation of the Cultural Revolution and Its Aftermath* (London: New Left Books, 1970). An additional point, however, needs to be made. No matter how limited the aim and scope of these mobilizations, they undoubtedly aided in politicizing the masses to a certain extent. The fact that the Chinese dissidents are, in their majority, Maoists can be traced to this turbulent period in Chinese politics. The cultural atrocities and loss of life dur-

ing the 'cultural revolution' should not lead us to unduly facile analogies with the Stalinist purges of the 1930s.

44 For an example of these, see Victor Serge, *Year One of the Russian Revolution* (London: Holt, Reinhart, and Winston, 1972).

45 Zhores Medvedev, 'Russia Under Brezhnev', *New Left Review*, 1(117) (September 1979): 3–29.

46 The 1977 Constitution abandoned all talk of soviets, even on paper. The Party was recognized as the only political organism of the state. Its membership had been just under 7 million in 1952 at the 19th Congress. At the 26th Congress in 1981 it stood at almost 18 million! The expansion was most noticeable in the collective farm sector and among industrial workers of the big towns. Thus any rise in social tensions or an outbreak of radical political demands would find an immediate reflection inside the CPSU itself.

47 Cited by the distinguished Sovietologist, Dr Bohdan Krawchenko of the University of Alberta, in a paper delivered to the Marx Centenary Conference in Winnipeg, Canada, March 1983.

48 Robin Blackburn, 'Fin de Siecle: Socialism after the Crash', *New Left Review*, 1(185) (January–February 1991): 5–66.

49 Hans Magnus Enzensberger, 'Karl Heinrich Marx', in *Selected Poems* (Michael Hamburger, Fred Viebhan and Rita Dove trans.) (Riverdale, NY: Sheep Meadow Press, 1999), pp. 55–8.

50 The latter turned out to be an admirer of Mussolini, to Ferguson's slight embarrassment.

51 Christopher A. Bayly, *The Birth of the Modern World, 1780–1914* (London: Blackwell, 2004). For a scholarly critique of this work by an economic historian, see Vivek Chibber, 'Sidelining the West?' *New Left Review*, 47 (September–October 2007): 130–41.

52 Emmet Larkin, Foreword to Jessica Prunty, *Dublin Slums, 1800–1925: A Study in Urban Geography* (Dublin: Irish Academic Press, 1998), p. ix. Quoted in Mike Davis, *Planet of Slums: Urban Involution and the Informal Working Class* (London: Verso, 2004), p. 10.

53 Davis, *Planet of Slums*, p. 10–11.

54 Giovanni Arrighi, 'The African Crisis', *New Left Review*, 15 (May–June 2002): 5–36.

55 Naomi Klein, *The Shock Doctrine: The Rise of Disaster Capitalism* (New York: Henry Holt, 2007).

56 R. H. Tawney, *Equality* (London: George, Allen & Unwin, 1964 [1931]).